T0384198

Cambridge Elements ≡

Elements in Gender and Politics
edited by
Tiffany D. Barnes
University of Texas at Austin
Diana Z. O'Brien
Washington University in St. Louis

WOMEN, GENDER, AND REBEL GOVERNANCE DURING CIVIL WARS

Meredith Maloof Loken
University of Amsterdam

CAMBRIDGE
UNIVERSITY PRESS

Shaftesbury Road, Cambridge CB2 8EA, United Kingdom

One Liberty Plaza, 20th Floor, New York, NY 10006, USA

477 Williamstown Road, Port Melbourne, VIC 3207, Australia

314–321, 3rd Floor, Plot 3, Splendor Forum, Jasola District Centre, New Delhi – 110025, India

103 Penang Road, #05–06/07, Visioncrest Commercial, Singapore 238467

Cambridge University Press is part of Cambridge University Press & Assessment, a department of the University of Cambridge.

We share the University's mission to contribute to society through the pursuit of education, learning and research at the highest international levels of excellence.

www.cambridge.org
Information on this title: www.cambridge.org/9781009494670

DOI: 10.1017/9781009335669

When citing this work, please include a reference to the DOI 10.1017/9781009335669

First published 2024

A catalogue record for this publication is available from the British Library

ISBN 978-1-009-49467-0 Hardback
ISBN 978-1-009-33567-6 Paperback
ISSN 2753-8117 (online)
ISSN 2753-8109 (print)

Additional resources for this publication at www.cambridge.org/loken_appendix

Women, Gender, and Rebel Governance during Civil Wars

Elements in Gender and Politics

DOI: 10.1017/9781009335669
First published online: December 2024

Meredith Maloof Loken
University of Amsterdam

Author for correspondence: Meredith Maloof Loken, m.m.loken@uva.nl

Abstract: How is rebel governance gendered, and how does women's participation in rebellion affect the development and execution of governance programs? The author develops a framework for evaluating and explaining rebel governance's gendered dynamics, identifying four areas where attention to women and to gender helps us better understand these institutions: recruitment and internal organization, program expansion, development of new projects, and multi-layered governance relationships. They explore the context and significance of these dynamics using cross-conflict data on rebel governance institutions and women's participation as well as qualitative evidence from three diverse organizations. They suggest that it is not only the fact of women's participation that matters but also the gendered nature of social and political relationships that help explain how rebels govern during civil wars. They show how women's involvement can shape governance content and implementation and how their participation may help rebel groups expand projects and engage with civilian communities.

Keywords: civil war, rebel governance, gender, rebellion, women

ISBNs: 9781009494670 (HB), 9781009335676 (PB), 9781009335669 (OC)
ISSNs: 2753-8117 (online), 2753-8109 (print)

Contents

An online appendix for this publication
can be accessed at www.cambridge.org/loken_appendix

1 Introduction: Gender and Rebellion during Civil Wars

In conflict-affected areas around the world, many rebel movements seek support and establish local control not only through violent attacks but through civilian outreach and governance efforts. Governance during war, by establishing non-military institutions like education, healthcare systems, schools, laws, and courts, can emphasize competence, demonstrate staying power, expand recruitment networks, integrate political ideas into local communities, and maintain or improve civilian life.[1] The pursuit of what Arjona calls "rebelocracy" – "situations of order where rebels intervene broadly in civilian affairs" – often leads armed groups to invest significantly in service provision and regulatory programs.[2]

Still, rebel governance operations vary significantly and not all organizations attempt such projects. A robust literature identifies and explains variation in governance institutions by highlighting group and conflict characteristics most associated with these programs. These include, but are not limited to, structural factors like state and rebel capacities, territorial control, domestic and international resources, and ideological and organizational factors like the desire for social transformation and nationalist agendas.[3] One key aspect of implementing governance is personnel capacity, the "human capital and human resources available to a rebel group[…] in non-kinetic activities, including those who are tasked with the governance missions of the organization."[4] This type of capacity encompasses individuals' "collective quality as reflected in their level of relevant expertise, experience, and training."[5] It is not only how many but *which* people participate in rebel governance that may be meaningfully related to governance outcomes.

For example, in Sri Lanka the Liberation Tigers of Tamil Eelam (LTTE)'s legal system was run by trained judges and lawyers whose incorporation of Tamil

---

[1] Megan A. Stewart, *Governing for Revolution: Social Transformation in Civil War* (Cambridge University Press, 2021); Zachariah Cherian Mampilly, *Rebel Rulers: Insurgent Governance and Civilian Life during War* (Cornell University Press, 2011); Ana Arjona, *Rebelocracy: Social Order in the Colombian Civil War* (Cambridge University Press, 2016).

[2] Arjona, *Rebelocracy*, 3.

[3] Ana Arjona, Nelson Kasfir, and Zachariah Mampilly, eds., *Rebel Governance in Civil War* (Cambridge University Press, 2015); Arjona, *Rebelocracy*; Reyko Huang and Patricia L. Sullivan, "Arms for Education? External Support and Rebel Social Services," *Journal of Peace Research* 58, no. 4 (2021): 794–808; Stewart, *Governing for Revolution*; Mara Redlich Revkin, "What Explains Taxation by Resource-Rich Rebels? Evidence from the Islamic State in Syria," *The Journal of Politics* 82, no. 2 (2020): 757–64; Niels Terpstra and Georg Frerks, "Rebel Governance and Legitimacy: Understanding the Impact of Rebel Legitimation on Civilian Compliance with the LTTE Rule," *Civil Wars* 19, no. 3 (2017): 279–307.

[4] Reyko Huang and Danielle F. Jung, "Capacity and Governance: Lessons from Rebels and States," in Cyanne E. Loyle, Jessica Braithwaite, Kathleen Cunningham, et al., "Revolt and Rule: Learning about Governance from Rebel Groups," *International Studies Review* 24, no. 4 (2022): 13.

[5] Ibid.

cultural norms into legal regulations helped legitimate the group's judicial agenda.[6] In other cases, civilians may see rebels' service provision as an act of solidarity when rebels share an ethnic group with the community,[7] but also when they do not. In Myanmar, the New Mon State Party (NMSP) reportedly derived some of its legitimacy, the "shared belief in the rightfulness of an armed group's agenda and activities,"[8] from its inclusive service provision wherein ethnic Mons administered not only to co-ethnic civilians, but the broader Mon State population.[9]

Gender constitutes an under-explored aspect of personnel capacity. This is significant because women are actively involved in rebellions and in governance across a diverse set of armed groups, because extant research emphasizes the importance of women's participation for rebel engagement with civilian populations, and because scholars document how rebels' internal gender dynamics can shape the nature and structure of their activities.[10] Yet we know relatively little about how women contribute to armed groups' governance efforts across civil wars and the effects that their participation can have on rebel behavior and relationships with civilians more broadly. Moreover, we can more deeply interrogate the *gendered dynamics* of these relationships, exploring how gendered expectations, norms, performances, and defiances within armed organizations are related to governance outcomes. In sum, what roles might gender play as a factor in rebels' relevant human capacities? How is rebel governance gendered, and how do these gendered dynamics affect the development and execution of governance programs?

This Element demonstrates that women make significant and gendered contributions to governance, that their participation can help shape the content and scope of these projects, and that women's spaces within armed movements are often sites of service provision for and oversight of civilians. Specifically, in this Element I develop a framework for assessing and explaining rebel governance's gendered dynamics. I detail the landscape of women's contributions to these institutions, offer theoretical and empirical insights into how and why women seek out governance roles and why rebels recruit them, and demonstrate how

---

[6] Mampilly, *Rebel Rulers*, 118.

[7] Ashley South, "'Hybrid Governance' and the Politics of Legitimacy in the Myanmar Peace Process," *Journal of Contemporary Asia* 48, no. 1 (2018): 50–66.

[8] Klaus Schlichte and Ulrich Schneckener, "Armed Groups and the Politics of Legitimacy," *Civil Wars* 17, no. 4 (2015): 410.

[9] Megan A. Stewart, "Civil War as State-Making: Strategic Governance in Civil War," *International Organization* 72, no. 1 (2018): 205–26.

[10] Phoebe Donnelly, "The Interactive Relationship between Gender and Strategy," *Global Society* 32, no. 4 (2018): 457–76; Meredith Loken, "Noncombat Participation in Rebellion: A Gendered Typology," *International Security* 47, no. 1 (2022): 139–70; Çağlayan Başer, "Women Insurgents, Rebel Organization Structure, and Sustaining the Rebellion: The Case of the Kurdistan Workers' Party," *Security Studies* 31, no. 3 (2022): 381–416; Hilary Matfess, *In Love and at War: Marriage in Non-state Armed Groups* (Cambridge University Press, Elements in Gender and Politics, 2024).

women's participation can both expand existing governance efforts and generate new programs that we would likely not observe in their absence.

After describing global associations between women's participation and governance institutions, I identify four individual but interrelated dynamics of rebel governance where attention to women and gender helps us better understand these programs: recruitment and internal organization, program expansion, development of new projects, and multi-layered governance relationships. I explore the context and significance of these dynamics in three diverse rebellions and demonstrate that it is not only the fact of women's participation that matters but the gendered nature of "how roles, responsibilities, and social relations are distributed and negotiated between men and women" that helps explain how rebel organizations govern.[11]

Research on rebel behavior is slow to consider how women's participation affects organizations beyond their military activities. The literature on women in rebellion also overwhelmingly focuses on frontline fighting roles; researchers pay relatively little attention at the comparative level to women's noncombatant contributions.[12] This work integrates these literatures and builds on existing scholarship on women, gender, and civil war to more deeply interrogate the gendered dynamics underpinning rebel efforts to govern civilian populations. The framework developed here relies on two key concepts from these fields: rebel governance and women's participation in rebellion. Therefore, in the remainder of this section I define and discuss these concepts as I use them in this Element. I draw together what we know about these wartime phenomena to explain why we should expect armed groups' gender dynamics to shape and be shaped by governance projects.

Rebel Governance

The contemporary statehood model holds that governments govern territory through a mix of protection, administration, service provision, accountability and punishment for legal violations, structural approval of specific social orders, and, in most cases, a military apparatus. In reality, control over these functions is usually divided among state and non-state actors. In areas of violent

---

[11] Zoe Marks, "Gender Dynamics in Rebel Groups," in *The Palgrave International Handbook of Gender and the Military*, ed. Rachel Woodward and Claire Duncanson (Palgrave Macmillan, 2017): 437.

[12] Exceptions include work that explores women's noncombatant participation within and across groups but within the same conflict or country. For example, see: Jenny Hedström, "Militarized Social Reproduction: Women's Labour and Parastate Armed Conflict," *Critical Military Studies* 1, no. 8 (2020): 58–76; Sarah Elizabeth Parkinson, "Organizing Rebellion: Rethinking High-Risk Mobilization and Social Networks in War," *The American Political Science Review* 107, no. 3 (2013): 418–32.

conflict this contestation is more extreme: armed, non-state organizations not only perform governmental functions, they also often assert authority over territory wrested from state control. For example, in Port-au-Prince, Haiti, local gangs and vigilante groups commit lethal, extralegal violence – lynchings – to hold individuals accountable for crimes and norm violations.[13] Inadequate performance of governance functions can engender a legitimacy crisis for states – in Port-au-Prince the population appears most supportive of these lynchings in areas with poor state governance and where the armed groups provide other services.[14]

During civil wars, such failures can create rich opportunities for rebellions seeking the authority that "statehood" provides, even if an autonomous state is not their ultimate goal. Rebel organizations are "consciously coordinated groups whose members engage in protracted violence with the intention of gaining undisputed political control over all or a portion of a pre-existing state's territory."[15] Many rebel organizations engage in governance, the "administration of civilian affairs" most often through rule-making, rule enforcement, and the provision of public goods and services.[16] Governance can demonstrate rebel viability as a state or rival armed group competitor, strengthen rebels' negotiation positions, enable violent groups to justify their agendas and actions by diversifying their activities beyond militancy, and help them gain domestic or international legitimacy and support. Rebels seek to demonstrate that they are capable bureaucrats and to soften perceptions that their movements are primarily or entirely violent without a sociopolitical vision for the future.[17]

Rebels face arduous journeys during civil wars and they rely on civilian support or acquiescence for resources, information, and survival. While some people share violent non-state groups' ideological and political beliefs, most people's preferences are more weakly held and are subject to the impacts of wartime shifts on their welfare.[18] Rebels can, and do, use violence to compel assistance from weakly affiliated civilians, but they risk backlash from a brutalized population. Therefore, rebels often try to convince civilians to assist with, endorse, or stay quiet about their activities through institutions, benefits, and other legitimacy-building enterprises. As Arjona and colleagues conclude,

> By creating systems of governance, rebels seek to win over local populations –
> or at least dissuade them from actively collaborating with incumbents. Such
> governance may deploy existing ideological or cultural beliefs that increase

---

[13] Danielle F. Jung and Dara Kay Cohen, *Lynching and Local Justice: Legitimacy and Accountability in Weak States* (Cambridge University Press, 2020).

[14] Ibid.   [15] Arjona, Kasfir, and Mampilly, eds., *Rebel Governance in Civil War,* 24.   [16] Ibid.

[17] Stewart, "Civil War as State-Making."

[18] Stathis N. Kalyvas, *The Logic of Violence in Civil War* (Cambridge University Press, 2006): 91.

identification with the insurgent cause. It may also provide goods and services that improve civilians' lives. At the same time, developing a governance capacity may also threaten existing authority structures and turn civilians against the rebellion. Rebel governance can, therefore, be a crucial factor in shaping the civilian–insurgent relationship. Insurgents who develop effective and legitimate governance systems can reap rewards, while those that fail often weaken their capacity to achieve their larger strategic objectives.[19]

Like other political actors, rebels need to "explain and justify their agendas and actions [...] Without minimal legitimacy, an armed group is bound to fail in its attempts to stay in power."[20] Successful governance institutions may suggest to observers that rebellions are not only powerful or viable, but that they are also the *right* political authorities when compared with the state or other actors.[21] This can help armed groups establish social control – access to people and their resources – even if groups are militarily weak or lack credentials in other areas.[22]

To these ends, organizations provide services in the form of food, medical care, utilities, security, welfare, or education; engage in diplomacy with international actors; and perform administrative functions like taxation and garbage collection. They create decision-making legislative bodies and hold elections. Rebels introduce their own laws, enforce them through policing, and adjudicate noncompliance through courts. Through these acts rebels "perform the state," projecting a narrative of infrastructural authority domestically and abroad.[23] Moreover, these arenas of legitimacy are linked through feedback effects wherein greater domestic legitimacy can enhance armed groups' international legitimacy, and vice versa.[24]

Research on the causes and effects of rebel governance concludes that these practices can produce tangible benefits. Rebels that provide services to civilians generally have more centralized organizational structures, which helps them organize and administer these kinds of programs and can signal administrative competence and bureaucracy to rival the state.[25] This narrative may reach not only civilians directly receiving those benefits but also the wider community, helping rebellions cultivate authority, legitimacy, and goodwill.[26] Indeed, rebels

---

[19] Arjona, Kasfir, and Mampilly, eds., *Rebel Governance in Civil War*, 3.

[20] Schlichte and Schneckener, "Armed Groups and the Politics of Legitimacy."

[21] Szekely, "Doing Well by Doing Good: Understanding Hamas's Social Services as Political Advertising," *Studies in Conflict & Terrorism* 38, no 4 (2015): 275–292.

[22] Corinna Jentzsch and Abbey Steele, "Social Control in Civil Wars," *Civil Wars* 25, no. 2–3 (2023): 452–71.

[23] José Ciro Martínez and Brent Eng, "Struggling to Perform the State: The Politics of Bread in the Syrian Civil War," *International Political Sociology* 11, no. 2 (2017): 133.

[24] Reyko Huang, "Rebel Diplomacy in Civil War," *International Security* 40, no. 4 (2016): 102.

[25] Lindsay L. Heger and Danielle F. Jung, "Negotiating with Rebels: The Effect of Rebel Service Provision on Conflict Negotiations," *Journal of Conflict Resolution* 61, no. 6 (2017): 1203–1229.

[26] Szekely, "Doing Well by Doing Good."

that provide public goods generally enjoy broader bases of support than those that do not engage in this type of governance.[27]

Some rebel groups administer a more interactive service to civilians: they hold elections wherein the community votes for their political representatives. As with other kinds of service provision, rebels pursuing local and international legitimacy, those with greater organizational capacity, and those most likely to engage in other kinds of civilian outreach appear most likely to hold elections.[28] Elections send a signal "that rebels aim to offer not only basic necessities but also a participatory order founded on popular inclusiveness" and that they are committed to political processes in addition to fighting.[29]

Another side of rebel governance disciplines the civilian population through laws and rules. These programs are not exclusively punitive – for example, rebels use laws and courts to address grievances, particularly those civilians hold against the state or rebels themselves, and create new rules that benefit from public approval.[30] But laws, policing, and courts also demonstrate the tangible authority of an organization that can secure compliance through the threat of punishment. In sum, by engaging in service provision, civilian administration, and regulating public order, rebellions can use local populations and territories to their advantage while generating support, recruits, and projecting an image of authority and, sometimes, righteousness.[31]

Some organizations control significant territory and regulate civilian life with no meaningful contestation from the state or other groups. Other rebels build parallel government structures and even administer justice without a proper monopoly on institutions or territorial control. Notably, governance practices and structures are not static; shifting conflict dynamics transform them throughout civil wars.[32] And governance systems, particularly those that seek to dramatically reform social orders, are not always popular among civilians who may resist or challenge them when they view pre-existing institutions as more effective or legitimate.[33] Still, governance efforts appear to generally strengthen rebellions in important ways and can result in tangible gains for armed organizations.[34]

[27] Heger and Jung, "Negotiating with Rebels."
[28] Kathleen Gallagher Cunningham, Reyko Huang, and Katherine M. Sawyer, "Voting for Militants: Rebel Elections in Civil War," *Journal of Conflict Resolution* 65, no. 1 (2021): 81–107.
[29] Ibid., 88.
[30] Cyanne E. Loyle, "Rebel Justice during Armed Conflict," *Journal of Conflict Resolution* 65, no. 1 (2021): 108–34.
[31] Cunningham, Huang, and Sawyer, "Voting for Militants," 86.   [32] Mampilly, *Rebel Rulers.*
[33] Arjona, Kasfir, and Mampilly, eds., *Rebel Governance in Civil War*; Gina Vale, "Defying Rules: Defying Gender?: Women's Resistance to Islamic State," *Studies in Conflict & Terrorism* 46, no. 6 (2023): 985–1008.
[34] Heger and Jung, "Negotiating with Rebels."

Women's Participation in Rebellion

In this Element I link rebel governance with women's participation in armed groups to argue that women's contributions can fundamentally affect and be affected by the character and objectives of governance projects. I focus specifically, therefore, on women's participation in *noncombatant work,* or work in and in support of organizations' logistical, administrative, social, and political apparatuses. Women take on noncombatant roles in the majority of rebellions and evidence from myriad conflicts suggests that their contributions are often an integral part of governing institutions. For example, women of the Khmer People's National Liberation Front (KPNLF), fighting against the People's Republic of Kampuchea regime in Cambodia, provided health services, childhood and adult literacy education, and domestic violence awareness programs to those living in KPNLF-controlled refugee camps.[35] Much of this work was done through the organization's women's wing, the Khmer Women's Association (KWA). One KPNLF woman noted in an interview with Dufresne, "We are women; we are in the background during this fighting. But women can operate together to rebuild our country. It is the women who will mend the social fabric."[36] Indeed, the KPNLF saw it as "politically important" that they "get credit for education provision rather than it going to outside forces," and the KWA's work demonstrated the KPNLF's interest in governance and concern for civilian welfare.[37]

Conceptually, in this project I follow Loken and Matfess' typology of roles within armed organizations – noncombatants, frontline fighters, and leaders (Table 1). These are not discrete categories, there is significant overlap. People often take on both frontline and noncombatant work throughout conflicts.[38] Similarly, leaders may compose military hierarchy or occupy high-ranking auxiliary, political, or social roles. But research also suggests that noncombatant labor makes up a consequential segment of rebel activity that is often separate from groups' military activities, and that noncombatant work may be distinctly gendered.[39]

---

[35] Jeffrey Robert Dufresne, "Rebuilding Cambodia: Education, Political Warfare, and the Khmer People's National Liberation Front" (Ph.D. dissertation, University of Saint Thomas, 1993); Stephen Clayton, "The Problem of 'Choice' and the Construction of the Demand for English in Cambodia," *Language Policy* 7 (2008): 143–64.

[36] Dufresne, "Rebuilding Cambodia," 277.

[37] Clayton, "The Problem of 'Choice' and the Construction of the Demand for English in Cambodia," 153.

[38] Many women who join rebellions are politicized by the groups' ideologies and objectives. Others seek economic resources or a new way of life, while others join to meet survival needs. Some are forcibly recruited. I consider women to be "participants in rebellion" when they work in service of the organization as a member or affiliate (self-identified or identified by the group) or in service of the organization's broader organs (political wings, for example) and are not identified by available sources as civilians.

[39] Loken, "Noncombat Participation in Rebellion."

Table 1 Definitional criteria for roles within rebel organizations, from Loken and Matfess (2022)[40]

Role	Criteria
Noncombatants	Activities involving identification with the structure, goals, ideology, or effort of the group and offering general supportive, noncombat labor; includes but is not limited to nurses, medics, cooks, spies, scouts, intelligence officers, smugglers, couriers, planners, administrators, recruiters, mobilizers, radio or weapons operators, guards, and camp followers; includes armed participants working in noncombat jobs
Frontline fighters	Activities involving participation in armed combat (including but not limited to the use of guns, grenades, bombs, and other weapons) and/or combat training; the perpetration of violence; or otherwise in the frontline environment in support of the group
Leaders	Activities involving the exercise of direct control over and provide oversight of other participants and/or exercise direct control over the strategy, policies, and/or ideology of the group; includes field commanders at all levels, military leadership at levels, and political leadership at all levels

For example, Parkinson explains how women kept Fatah viable in Lebanon in the 1980s through mobilization and logistical work. She notes that women "could 'naturally' congregate in salons, which consequently became hubs of underground political activity" because women attracted less suspicion from security forces.[41] Women exploited these stereotypes as effective couriers and logisticians. In Northern Ireland, women drove with male Provisional Israeli Republican Army (Provisional IRA) fighters over the Republic of Ireland border to smuggle weapons and messages and to transport fighters. They posed as wives, sometimes even bringing children with them, to dispel suspicion from the border guards. Some women volunteered for this job because, as

[40] Meredith Loken and Hilary Matfess, *Women's Activities in Armed Rebellion (WAAR) Project Dataset v1.0 Codebook* (2022): 9.
[41] Sarah Elizabeth Parkinson, *Beyond the Lines: Social Networks and Palestinian Militant Organizations in Wartime Lebanon* (Cornell University Press, 2022), 71–72.

former participants recall, such work allowed them to contribute to the struggle while also being available for family obligations.[42] Governance work may be a similarly unique form of gendered noncombatant labor. For example, women may take on responsibilities for some kinds of governance, like education and welfare provisioning, "because they generally already occupy positions in the home or the labor force related to these services" and because they see opportunities for themselves in or are expected to perform these kinds of work due to pre-existing gendered divisions of labor.[43]

Women participate within rebel movements not only as individuals but also collectively within all-women's organizations. Women's wings are common: about a third of rebel groups sampled by the Women's Activities in Armed Rebellion (WAAR) Project included women's wings primarily engaged in noncombatant work, while some also included women's combat units.[44] Some women's wings are internally-focused on providing logistical support to fighters, but many primarily engage with the broader population. Women's wings advance political agendas and fundraise, and they are often primary provisioners of services to civilians like education and welfare. Women's wings can be forums for women to push rebel management on gendered issues, exercise agency, leadership, and policy-making, as well as carve out a space for themselves in rebellion. They can also be restrictive organizations where rebel leaders sideline women members.[45] In this project I focus on women's spaces within rebel groups and their roles in facilitating, expanding, and developing governance programs because they are often sites of mobilization and rebel engagement with civilians.

A final, important consideration is the work that women civilians do during war to self-govern their communities in the absence or contestation of state and/or rebel rule. Sometimes such work is a form of noncooperation, conducted in defiance of armed groups.[46] But often these activities persist alongside or in coordination with rebel agendas, among those who both are and are not supporters of the armed organizations. Hedström, for example, introduces the concept of "militarized social reproduction," "the everyday emotional, material, and symbolic labour

---

[42] *Cumann na mBan: The Women's Army* (Indiana University – Purdue University Indianapolis (IUPUI) University Library, 2019), https://ulib.iupui.edu/video/CumannnamBan.

[43] Loken, "Noncombat Participation in Rebellion," 154.

[44] Hilary Matfess and Meredith Loken, "Women's Wings in Rebel Organisations: Prevalence, Purposes and Variations," *Civil Wars* (2024): 1–27. https://doi.org/10.1080/13698249.2024.2302737.

[45] Ibid.

[46] Juan Masullo, "Refusing to Cooperate with Armed Groups Civilian Agency and Civilian Noncooperation in Armed Conflicts," *International Studies Review* 23, no. 3 (2021): 887–913; Vale, "Defying Rules: Defying Gender? "

undertaken by women within the household and the non-state or parastate armed group in communities embroiled in civil wars."[47] This labor can underwrite rebel governance when civilians work with or in support of rebel goals; for example, civilian women living alongside the Farabundo Martí National Liberation Front (FMLN) in El Salvador provided medical care for other civilians and for rebellion participants.[48] But in other cases civilians engage in self-help governance alongside but not necessarily in collaboration with armed groups. Moreover, the boundaries between participant and civilian, activist and observer, are often not neatly defined. I explore the complex dynamics of this multi-layered governance more deeply in this Element, as governance and the civilian-combatant distinction are both gendered and relevant for understanding rebel behavior.

By focusing on the gendered dynamics of rebel governance, this Element contributes to the literature exploring how, when, and where women's activities are tangibly related to rebel behavior and outcomes. This body of scholarship focuses primarily on women frontline fighters; we know, for example, that women's participation on the frontline impacts conflict duration, informs military strategies, influences external support for rebellions, impacts the peace bargaining process, and is associated with how civil wars end.[49] I attend exclusively in this Element to women's noncombatant work, which appears uniquely associated with and significant for rebel governing institutions, to demonstrate how women's contributions to the "rest of rebellion" are also directly and indirectly consequential for armed movements.

Research Strategy and Outline of the Element

In this Element, I explore two broad questions: how is rebel governance gendered and how do these gendered dynamics shape the content and execution of governance programs? To answer these questions I employ a descriptive research strategy that illustrates patterns across civil wars, offers a framework

---

[47] Jenny Hedström, "Militarized Social Reproduction: Women's Labour and Parastate Armed Conflict," *Critical Military Studies* 8, no. 1 (2022): 58–76.

[48] Jocelyn Viterna, *Women in War: The Micro-Processes of Mobilization in El Salvador* (Oxford University Press, 2013).

[49] Alex Braithwaite and Luna B. Ruiz, "Female Combatants, Forced Recruitment, and Civil Conflict Outcomes," *Research & Politics* 5, no. 2 (2018): 1–9; Jakana L. Thomas, "Wolves in Sheep's Clothing: Assessing the Effect of Gender Norms on the Lethality of Female Suicide Terrorism," *International Organization* 75, no. 3 (2021): 769–802; Keshab Giri and Roos Haer, "Female Combatants and Durability of Civil War," *Studies in Conflict & Terrorism* 47, no. 5 (2024): 526–47; Elizabeth L. Brannon, Jakana Thomas, and Lora DiBlasi, "Fighting for Peace? The Direct and Indirect Effects of Women's Participation in Rebel Groups on Peace Negotiations," *The Journal of Politics* 86, no. 2 (2024): 1–14; Lindsey A. Goldberg, "International Virtue Signaling: How Female Combatants Shape State Support for Armed Rebellion," *Conflict Management and Peace Science* (2024): 1–24. https://doi.org/10.1177/07388942241234224.

for studying and understanding these relationships, and uses this framework to explore and explain gendered governance in specific contexts.

In Section 2, I first lay out what we know about the empirical relationships between rebel governance institutions and women's noncombatant participation during civil wars. I use cross-conflict, quantitative data to identify patterns at the global level. I demonstrate that across rebel groups in the post-World War II period, rebel service provision and regulatory governance institutions are strongly associated with women's participation (if women participate in the group in noncombatant roles), the relative prevalence of women's participation (the estimated proportion of women participants in noncombatant roles relative to all those participating in this way), and the presence of women's noncombatant wings.

Section 3 develops a framework to help explain these associations and gendered governance more broadly. I identify four consequential dynamics of gendered armed group governance – (1) recruitment and internal organization, (2) program expansion, (3) development of new projects, and (4) multi-layered governance – and argue that attention to these factors help us better understand and explain governance practices. I offer evidence for co-constitutive relationships rather than mono-directional causal ones: I show how women's involvement can shape governance content and implementation, how their participation may help rebel groups expand projects and influence external views of their activities, and how governance efforts may simply require rebels to develop more robust human capacities to enact their agendas.

In Section 4, I use this framework to describe how these dynamics of gendered governance manifest in three rebellions that fought in different civil wars: the Islamic State (IS) in Iraq and Syria, the Revolutionary Front for an Independent East Timor (Fretilin) in East Timor (now Timor Leste), and the Provisional IRA in Northern Ireland. I examine how women's recruitment, participation in governance expansion and development, and engagement from below affects and is affected by rebel governance practices in these contexts. These cases broadly account for key structural and sociocultural variation that may be consequential for both rebel governance and for women's participation.

In this section, I use primary source data for analyses related IS collected from IS propaganda outlets between 2015 and 2016, from Aymenn Jawad Al-Tamimi's archives, and from Jihadology. Primary source data concerning Northern Ireland draws on original data from my field research over three trips between 2017 and 2022. This includes interviews with former Provisional IRA participants, republican activists, and civilians in Belfast

and Derry and archival material housed in the Linen Hall Library and Eileen
Hickey Irish Republican History Museum.[50] The Fretilin analysis relies on
only secondary data sources.

Finally, Section 5 overviews the Element's arguments and findings and
discusses the implications of this research, calling attention to the "so what"
of this project. I illustrate how the relationships and patterns identified here can
help us understand the consequences and legacies of rebel governance, including through reintegration practices and rebel-to-party transitions. I also discuss
future avenues of study that this project presents for scholarship on gendered
rebel governance.

2 Identifying Global Patterns

I first turn to examining patterns of relationships between rebel governance
institutions and women's noncombatant participation at the cross-conflict level.
I do not develop an explanation for cross-conflict variation or advance a mono-
causal, directional argument in this project, but I use these empirical trends to
ground theoretical and empirical interrogation of how governance is gendered,
how attention to women and gender can help explain these patterns, and what
this means for rebel activities and outcomes.

Data Sources and Sampling Strategy

I rely on two datasets to define the scope of my data sample. For data on rebel
governance, I use the Rebel Quasi-State Institutions (RQSI) dataset, which
offers yearly data on 234 rebels groups' governing institutions between 1945
and 2012.[51] These data measure if a rebel group engaged in the institution in a
given year and I collapse them into dichotomous measures of if a group ever
engaged in a governance institution. From the RQSI dataset, I draw data on the
governance institutions most commonly discussed in the rebel governance
literature. Four of these variables, *education, healthcare, welfare/aid,* and
elections for civilian government positions, capture service provision projects.
Three variables capture regulatory programs, *laws over civilian behavior,
justice systems,* and *policing.*[52] I also include the RQSI measure for *diplomacy,*
which captures rebel governance efforts aimed internationally. I include eight

---

[50] This research was carried out as part of University of Washington IRB ID MOD00000119.
[51] Karen E. Albert, "What Is Rebel Governance? Introducing a New Dataset on Rebel Institutions,
1945–2012," *Journal of Peace Research* 59, no. 4 (2022): 622–30. The RQSI documentation
notes that the dataset includes 235 rebel groups, but there are 234 unique UCDP actor codes in
the data.
[52] See the Online Appendix for coding descriptions for these variables, retrieved from Karen E.
Albert, *Rebel Quasi-State Dataset Codebook* (2020).

institutional measures to account for the broad scope of governance and for potential relational differences between women's participation and specific governance outcomes.

I use data on women's participation in rebel organizations from the WAAR Project version 1.0. Women's Activities in Armed Rebellion Project data offers group-level, time invariant measures of women's reported participation across multiple variables for 372 rebellions operating between 1946 and 2015.[53] This includes data on women's noncombatant, frontline, and leadership activities. Neither the WAAR Project nor other available sources collect data specifically on women's participation in governance roles, but the WAAR Project provides data on three related measures that I use to capture underlying relationships.[54] These assess women's noncombatant contributions: noncombatant activities are expansive and include work such as combat medicine and spying, but this work also includes many aspects of rebel governance, including service and goods provision like educating civilians or working in administrative offices, policing and rule enforcement, and political participation in rule-making rebel bodies. *Noncombatant participation* measures whether a rebel group includes women in visible noncombatant roles (0/1). *Noncombatant prevalence* estimates the prevalence of women's participation in these roles relative to the groups' membership. It is coded on an ordinal scale from 0 to 4: no/unverified, occasional, low, moderate, or widespread participation. For example, "moderate" participation indicates that women composed between 10 percent and 19 percent of visible noncombatant participants within an organization. *Women's noncombatant wings* captures when rebel groups included at least one women's wing whose primary work was focused on noncombatant activities (0/1).[55]

Overlapping cases between these two datasets produce a sample of 194 rebellions across 60 countries used in this Element.[56] This sample represents almost perfectly the distribution of governance institutions in the full RQSI dataset (Table 2). For example, 32 percent of rebellions for which there is data

[53] Meredith Loken and Hilary Matfess, "Introducing the Women's Activities in Armed Rebellion (WAAR) Project, 1946–2015," *Journal of Peace Research* 61, no. 3 (2023): 489–99.

[54] See the Online Appendix for coding descriptions for these variables, retrieved from Loken and Matfess, *Women's Activities in Armed Rebellion (WAAR) Project Dataset v1.0 Codebook* (2022).

[55] Collecting systematic measures of women's participation in rebellion is difficult, in part because this requires quantifying largely qualitative information with few precise measures. This is particularly true of efforts to assess women's *noncombatant* participation: Noncombatant women may be disregarded by documenters as simply "not fighters" or civilians, they may be less visible as many do not work on the frontlines, and their work may be purposefully clandestine. Therefore, these measures are assessments of visibility in available sources, not exact estimates. The WAAR Project identifies women's participation as *verified* or *not verified* – it is likely that women participate more widely than documented.

[56] See the Online Appendix for a list of organizations included in the sample and visualizations of women's participation and rebel governance across groups.

Table 2 Percent of rebel groups that engage
in each governance institution[57]

	RQSI	**Sample**
Education	32	34
Healthcare	28	29
Aid	17	17
Elections	14	14
Law	31	30
Policing	28	29
Justice	30	30
Diplomacy	17	18

Table 3 Percent of rebel groups that include visible women in
each role[58]

	WAAR Project	**Sample**
Noncombatants	59	69
Frontline fighters	53	63
Women's noncombatant wings	32	42

in the RQSI dataset provided education to civilians, compared with 34 percent in the combined data sample. But the overlapping cases oversample women's participation in rebel groups relative to the full universe of cases in the WAAR Project dataset (Table 3).[59] There is a significant difference of approximately ten percentage points across different types of women's participation.

One explanation is that the RQSI dataset may over-sample rebellions coded as women-inclusive relative to possible cases. The RQSI dataset includes only groups from the UCDP/PRIO's Armed Conflict Termination dataset also involved in civil wars that "caused at least 1,000 battle-deaths."[60] The WAAR Project dataset draws its sample from the UCDP Dyadic Dataset v1.2015 but does not use the same total battle-deaths threshold as RQSI. Conflicts at the

[57] RQSI *n* = 229; Sample *n* = 191.
[58] WAAR *n* = 370 except for women's noncombatant wings data, where *n* = 367; Sample *n* = 192 except for women's noncombatant wings data, where *n* = 189.
[59] In this Element, all descriptive statistics refer to complete cases without missing data. Footnotes detail the respective "*n*"s. All percentages are rounded.
[60] Albert, "What Is Rebel Governance?" 624.

scale of inclusion for the RQSI dataset are more lethal, may be longer, and include larger or more capable groups. Research suggests that women-inclusive rebellions are larger and more durable than other organizations.[61] It is therefore likely that more scholarly and reporting attention has been paid to rebel groups included in RQSI relative to other cases, including many also in the WAAR Project data. This includes attention to and recording of women's activities. Therefore, I suspect that the data sample of overlapping rebellions used here likely over-samples stronger, more durable, more women-inclusive, and better documented rebel groups relative to the full universe of possible cases.

Evaluating these measures of rebel governance and women's participation in rebellions reveal temporal trends. Figures 1 and 2 present the distribution of these variables across time using data on the decade in which a rebellion began fighting.[62] In this sample, rebel groups that include women in visible noncombatant roles outnumber other organizations in most years and women's participation does not appear to vary significantly over time (Figure 1). But these data do suggest a decline in the presence of women's wings among groups that began fighting at the end of the twentieth century (Figure 1). This "may reflect the waning influence of leftist ideology as an inspiration for rebel groups emerging after the end of the Cold War and the relative rise of religiously-motivated organisations. It is also possible that greater norm diffusion and developments in women's rights and roles across the globe have publicised and normalised women's participation in rebel groups, resulting in greater integration of women and men in the same units."[63]

The distribution of governance-engaging rebellions appears fairly even over time (Figure 2). Rebels providing services to civilians made up the largest proportion of groups in some decades, perhaps due to the smaller number of rebellions that began fighting in those decades, but generally the minority of organizations engage in this kind of governance. This pattern also holds true for regulatory governance and diplomatic efforts (Figure 2).

Exploring the Relationships between Rebel Governance and Women's Participation

There are clear associations between whether rebels in this dataset engage in governance programs and if they include women noncombatants. This descriptive

---

[61] Jakana L. Thomas and Kanisha D. Bond, "Women's Participation in Violent Political Organizations," *American Political Science Review* 109, no. 3 (2015): 488–506; Giri and Haer, "Female Combatants and Durability of Civil War."

[62] "Fight decade" data is from the Foundations of Rebel Group Emergence (FORGE) Dataset, 1946–2011, Jessica Maves Braithwaite, and Kathleen Gallagher Cunningham, "When Organizations Rebel: Introducing the Foundations of Rebel Group Emergence (FORGE) Dataset," International Studies Quarterly 64, no. 1 (2020): 183–93.

[63] Matfess and Loken, "Women's Wings in Rebel Organisations," 7.

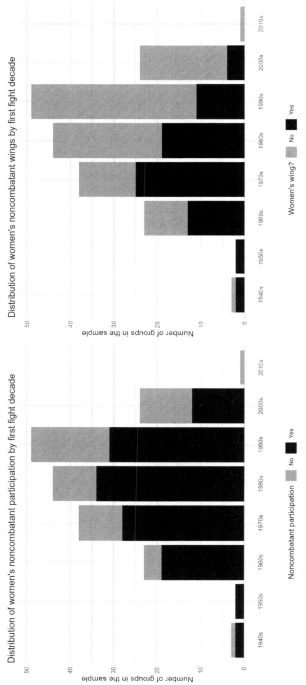

Figure 1 Distribution of women's participation variables over time[64]

---

[64] $n = 184$.

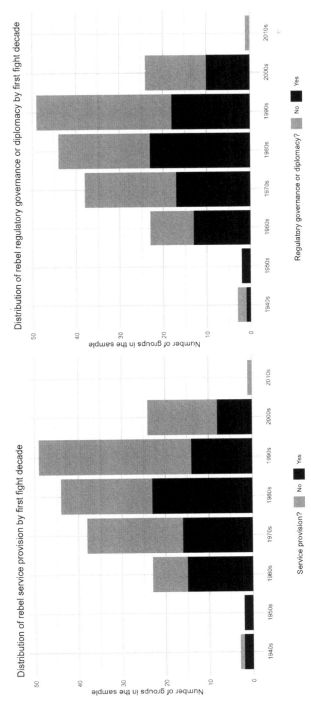

Figure 2 Distribution of rebel governance variables over time[65]

[65] *n* = 184.

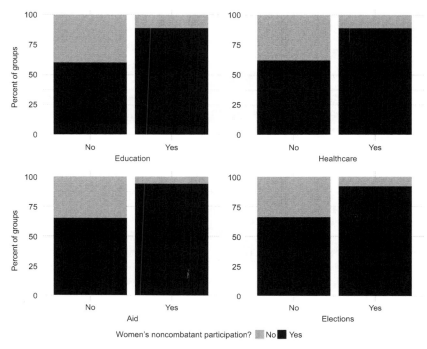

Figure 3 Distribution of women's participation by
if rebels provided services to civilians[66]

trend spans the governance institutions studied, as Figures 3 and 4 illustrate. Rebellions engaged in service provision, civilian regulation and management, and/or international diplomatic efforts are markedly more inclined to incorporate women compared to rebellions not offering similar services or engaging in analogous activities.

Consider rebels' provision of welfare aid (Figure 3). An observed 35 percent of groups abstaining from aid provision also exclude women from noncombatant roles, while 65 percent of such groups include women in their ranks. But if we focus only on rebellions providing aid, only 6 percent exhibit no visible female noncombatant involvement, contrasting with the nearly 94 percent inclusion rate. Turning to rebels' regulatory institutions (Figure 4), 41 percent of rebellions without their own laws also lack noncombatant women, compared to 59 percent of groups not engaged in legal activities but including women in these roles. However, among groups enacting laws over civilians, 95 percent include women as noncombatants, with only five percent excluding them. These patterns

---

[66] $n = 189$.

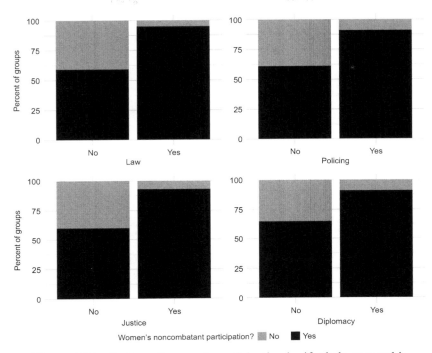

Figure 4 Distribution of women's participation by if rebels engaged in regulatory and/or diplomatic institutions[67]

highlight the associational relationships between governance activities and the involvement of women in rebel groups.

As Figures 3 and 4 suggest, these distributions are similar across different types of governance institutions. Correlational data indicates that while some governance institutions are related to each other (e.g., provision of health-care is strongly correlated with provision of education), most institutions enjoy moderate to weak correlations with one another.[68] This means that the similarity in relationships across governance types cannot only be explained by co-occurrence of governance programs within and across rebellions.

I am interested not only in the relationships between the fact of women's noncombatant participation and rebel governance, but also in how the *prevalence* of women's participation is associated with these institutions. Is rebels' probability of engaging in governance associated with the proportion of women in the group? To explore the relationship between women's participation levels and governance programs, I employ logistic regression models to calculate the odds ratios associated with the known prevalence of women in noncombatant

---

[67] $n = 189$.   [68] See the Online Appendix for correlational data.

roles. These ratios compare each level of women's participation in noncombatant roles with no/unverified participation (coded as 0) across various institutions. To account for dependencies, standard errors are clustered based on the
rebels' primary operational country. These are descriptive analyses that do not
include confounding variables.

These results are visualized in Figure 5. In this figure, the estimate for *none* (no/
unverified participation) serves as the baseline odds – the likelihood of rebel
groups engaging in the governance institution when noncombatant women are
not participating.[69] The dotted line marks an odds ratio of 1, representing chance.
If the confidence intervals intersect this line, it suggests that the observed effect
size is not significantly different from "no effect" in the population. An odds ratio
greater than 1 indicates that a higher proportion of women in the group is more
likely to be associated with rebels engaging in governance, while an odds ratio
less than 1 indicates the opposite.

There are no cases in these data where women's noncombatant participation
is coded as *occasional* in the *noncombatant prevalence* variable. Therefore,
there is no estimate calculated in this analysis for that category and it is excluded
in the visualizations.

These findings highlight a general association between the level of women's
noncombatant participation and the probability that rebels engage in various governance programs. However, the strength of these associations differs among
institutions, particularly regarding the odds of engagement for groups with *low*
prevalence of women. For instance, the odds of a group providing healthcare when
they do not include women noncombatants is approximately 0.12 (baseline odds).
The odds ratio for a group with a *low* level of women's noncombatant participation
providing healthcare is estimated to be 3.8 times higher than the baseline odds.
However, the confidence intervals for this coefficient include the value 1 (cross the
line), suggesting uncertainty about the true effect size. Therefore, although the
coefficient suggests a positive relationship, the overlapping confidence intervals
prevent us from confidently labeling this as a statistically significant effect. The
odds for a group with *moderate* or *high* levels of women's participation providing
healthcare are 5.7 and 9.2 times greater than the baseline odds, respectively. These
are highly statistically significant associations.

Because of the wide confidence intervals for these results and the lack of
confounding variables, it is difficult to know if the odds of governance grows
consecutively relative to the baseline odds as the proportion of women
increases, though the coefficient estimates suggest this is at least possible in

---

[69] The variable is an ordinal variable but in the model it is treated as a series of dummy contrasts,
comparing each level to the baseline. See the Online Appendix for the full logistic regression
results.

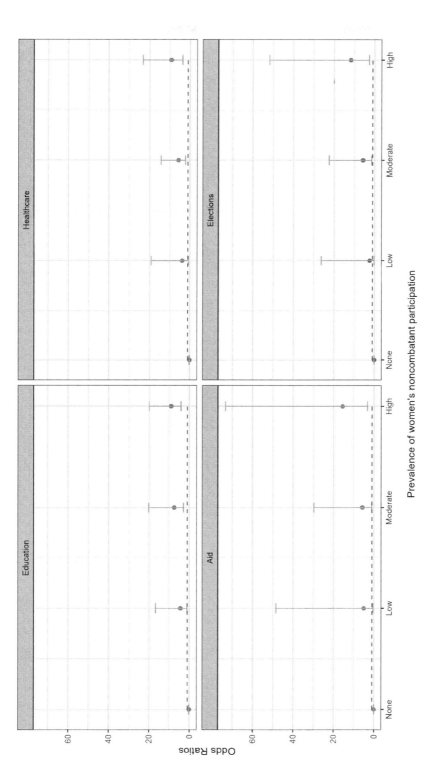

Figure 5 Odds ratios of a group engaging in each governance institution for each level of women's participation compared with no/unverified participation[70]

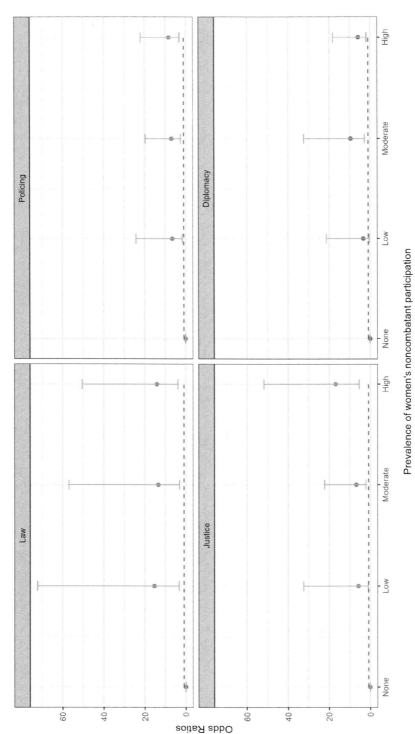

Prevalence of women's noncombatant participation

Figure 5 (cont.)

most cases. For example, in some models including *aid* and *elections, moderate* and *high* levels of women's participation are associated with the governance institutions at statistically significant points ($p < 0.05$, $p < 0.001$), but the *low* level of participation is not. Future research considering the direction of these relationships and covariates may examine and explain variation across institutions and the prevalence of women noncombatants. But these results do make clear that women's noncombatant participation at all levels, but especially moderate and high levels, appears significantly associated with rebels' engagement in governance across institutions.

As I discuss in Section 1, women often participate in rebellions within women's noncombatant wings. These units are where women's leadership and decision-making positions are often best represented, and they are often core sites for civilian outreach. I therefore examine the associational relationships between governance institutions and women's wings, and I look specifically at service provision institutions as they are theoretically most related to these kinds of civilian engagement (Figure 6).[71]

The odds of rebel organizations providing education, healthcare, welfare aid, and holding civilian elections are significantly higher when the groups include women's noncombatant wings. For example, the odds that a group with at least one women's wing provided education to civilians are approximately 3.88 times greater than for organizations without women's units. If we look at the underlying data, we can see these associations represented in the descriptive statistics as well: 69 percent of groups not providing education lack a women's wing while 31 percent of such groups include a women's unit. Of rebellions that do engage in education, 63 percent have a women's wing compared with 37 percent that do not. These distributions are similar across institutions.

I suggest that women's noncombatant work is unique and uniquely important for rebel governance. But though this Element focuses on women noncombatants, it is important to also consider noncombatants as part of the whole of women's participation. Their mobilization, recruitment, positions, and activities compose a piece of rebellions' broader gendered strategies and gendered dynamics. It is not only noncombatants who contribute to rebel projects. Therefore, I briefly examine patterns in the cross-conflict environment comparing noncombatants to frontline fighters to explore the distinctiveness of noncombatant labor in the governance context. I compare associations across two kinds of governance: education, emblematic of service provision and therefore most likely associated with noncombatants compared with frontline fighters, and policing, a regulatory form of

---

[71] See the Online Appendix for the full logistic regression results.

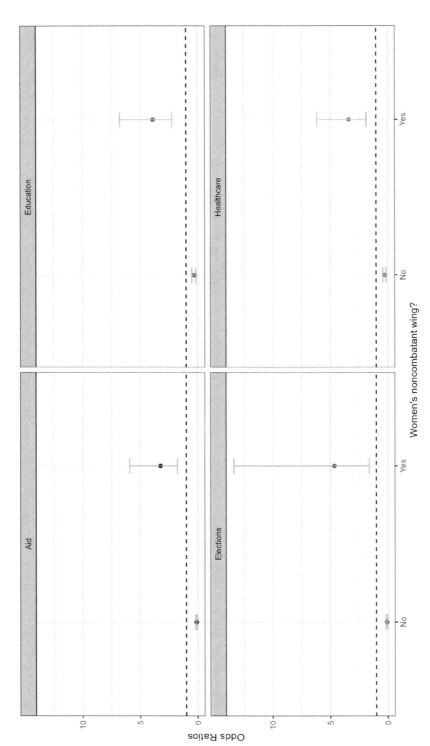

Figure 6 Odds ratios of rebellions with women's wings engaging in each governance institution compared with no/unverified women's units[72]

---

[72] $n = 186$.

governance that, while not a combat activity, is the closest form of governance to fighting and often involves armed participants.

In both cases, governance programs appear more associated with women's noncombatant participation than frontline involvement (Figures 7 and 8). For example, over 90 percent of rebels engaged in policing also recruit women noncombatants, while approximately 80 percent of those in this group incorporate women frontline fighters. Future research may explore the differences across women's participation type in this context more thoroughly.

These brief analyses do not examine every relationship between governance institutions and women's participation in rebellion. I intend them only to describe the general, global landscape. But these data demonstrate clear associations between rebellions engaging in governance and women's noncombatant activities. Moreover, they suggest that it is not only women's presence that is related to rebel governance but also possibly the relative level of women's participation and

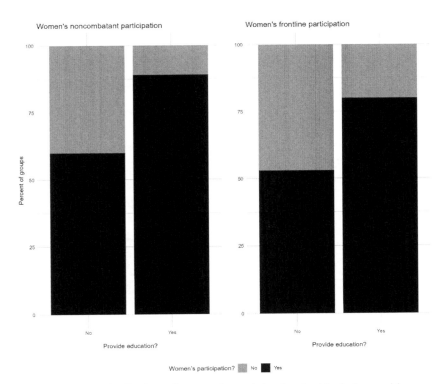

Figure 7 Distribution of women's participation by if rebels provide education to civilians[73]

---

[73] $n = 189$.

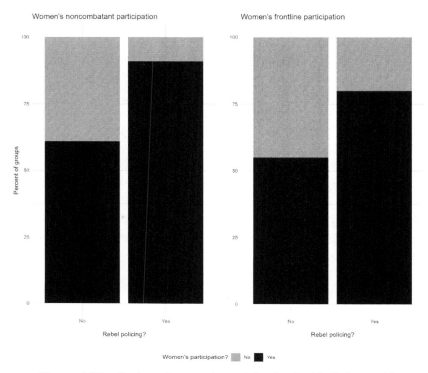

Figure 8 Distribution of women's participation by if rebels provide
policing for intra-civilian relations[74]

the operation of women's wings within organizations that matter. How might we
explain these associations? Why might rebellions engaged in governance be
generally more likely to include women and women's units?

In the next section, I develop a framework for exploring the gendered
dynamics of rebel governance during civil wars. I suggest that women's recruitment and participation in noncombatant roles offers rebellions benefits that
include the expansion and development of governance programs. I also demonstrate how women's involvement and rebel governance may be co-occurring
factors in rebels' broader organizational agendas.

3 Gendering Rebel Governance

I identify four individual but interrelated dynamics of rebel governance where
attention to women and gender helps us better understand these practices:
(1) recruitment and internal organization, who is recruited into rebels' non-
fighting apparatuses, where, and why; (2) governance expansion, how women's

---

[74] $n = 189.$

participation in rebel groups can contribute to and expand existing or planned rebel programs; (3) governance development, how women create new governance programs or change existing ones in unique ways; and (4) multi-layered governance, how civilian women's involvement in governance "from below" relates to rebel governance and requires us to re-think non-state governance beyond a singular focus on rebel administration. This framework gives rise to two co-constitutive arguments that help explain and contextualize the positive associations identified in Section 2. First, women's participation can provide direct benefits to rebel governance initiation, expansion, and development through community engagement and access as well as through legitimacy cultivation. Second, as governance institutions grow in size and ambition, rebellions require more human capacity to maintain them and may recruit more women accordingly.

These four dynamics are all discrete parts of rebellions but they are not mutually exclusive. I discuss each separately, but these are relational categories. For example, how women are recruited and organized within rebel groups likely also affects their desire and ability to establish new governance programs or to expand existing ones. Women often administer leadership-planned programs *and* create new ones. And importantly, these dynamics are not all present or meaningfully gendered in every rebellion. But, taken together, attention to them helps us better understand the shape and scope of rebel governance.

Recruitment and Internal Organization

Who is recruited into rebels' governing apparatuses, where, and why? Gender likely plays a role in recruitment into governance work in two related ways. First, from a demand perspective, some rebellions may recruit women specifically into these roles because of pre-war gendered socialization and norms that make women particularly well-prepared to administer some programs, like education, and that can provide inimitable access to civilian communities. The normalization of militarization in society, including through armed actors' engagement with civilians, does not "just occur," it is closely managed by armed groups.[75] Rebels may also view recruiting women into governance roles not only as tangibly beneficial but also symbolically important as a method of building legitimacy around gendered narratives.[76] Second, from a supply perspective, governance work may attract and create new opportunities for women to develop what Viterna calls a "participant identity," defined as participating in a movement because it "seems like a natural and even necessary thing

---

[75] Hedström, "Militarized Social Reproduction."

[76] Hilary Matfess and Robert U. Nagel, "Women and Rebel Legitimacy," Policy Roundtable: How Gender Affects Conflict and Security (Texas National Security Review, 2020), https://tnsr.org/roundtable/policy-roundtable-gender-and-security/; Goldberg, "International Virtue Signaling."

for 'people like [you]' to do."[77] As I discuss below, this may be due in part to how women organize within and alongside armed organizations and the work of women's wings as governance administrators in many groups. These two pathways into rebellion likely operate cyclically: as rebellions recruit women, other women may see greater opportunities to participate, and as more women participate in rebellions, rebels may seek to compound on the advantages they provide. Armed groups that include women are usually larger and more durable than other organizations, offering them resources and time to develop stronger, more robust organizational and human capacities as well as relationships with civilian communities and international actors.[78]

First, women often participate in rebellions in ways similar to their pre-war sociopolitical, economic, and community roles. Traditional divisions of labor, coupled with historical exclusion from and/or restrictions on women's participation in formal politics in most societies, means that women most often contribute to rebel organizations in auxiliary, administrative, and social roles.[79] Much of this is work that directly supports fighting, such as spying, weapons carrying, and attack planning, but much of it is also encapsulated by what Hedström calls "everyday work […] materially enabling armed conflict" within and in support of armed movements: tending to civilian and combatant life off of the front-line.[80] Women's contributions, then, may better equip rebel groups to provide aspects of governance that overlap with the traditionally "domestic" sphere, including education, healthcare, and broader welfare initiatives where women may already disproportionately engage with the civilian population. Rebel leadership, in turn, may recognize this potential for mobilization and expansion and recruit women specifically into such roles.

For example, the Karen National Union (KNU) in Myanmar created in its early years a women's wing, the Karen Women's Organization (KWO) and reportedly restricted its mandate to service provision and social welfare. According to Israelsen, the KWO's purpose "was to support the participation of women in the KNU's mission to establish a sovereign state and then later in the 1970s, a federal system of government within the Burmese state," but instead they largely provided for the civilian community and cared for war orphans on the KNU's behalf.[81]

---

[77] Jocelyn Viterna, *Women in War*, 51.

[78] Thomas and Bond, "Women's Participation in Violent Political Organizations"; Giri and Haer, "Female Combatants and Durability of Civil War."

[79] Leena Vastapuu, "Beans, Bullets and Bandages? Gendered and Racialised Othering in the Depiction of Military Support Work," *Civil Wars* (2023): 1–21. https://doi.org/10.1080/13698249.2023.2247777; Loken, "Noncombat Participation in Rebellion."

[80] Hedström, "Militarized Social Reproduction," 8.

[81] Shelli Israelsen, "Women in Charge: The Effect of Rebel Governance and Women's Organisations on Karen Women's Political Participation," *Civil Wars* 20, no. 3 (2018): 379–407.

It was not until the KWO gained more independence and autonomy from KNU leadership nearly forty years after its creation that the group "radically re-oriented" itself away from exclusive service provision and toward women's political participation, education, and social and state liberation.[82]

Rebel leadership may also view engagement with civilians as an important method of legitimizing and integrating militants into society, and governance may be a powerful device for rebels engaged in gendered reputation-building. This is for two intersecting reasons: domestic and international audiences may confer more legitimacy onto armed groups when women participate because women's involvement can make groups seem less like fringe extremists and more like inclusive, righteous political organizations[83]; and governance is a primary way that organizations "can strengthen civilian perceptions of group legitimacy which in turn influences civilian mobilization and support."[84] For these reasons, we may expect civilian-intensive initiatives like holding elections or regulatory governance and women's participation to be co-occurring phenomena.

Rebel mobilization and governance also often take place in civilian spaces – homes, towns with majority female-headed households, schools, refugee camps – where women may be most welcome and best integrated. For example, research on information spread within social, ethnic networks – where rumors of or information about rebellion are generally shared – concludes that women are significantly more likely to hear news from such networks than men.[85] Women, then, may offer rebellions opportunities to engage with civilians where there may otherwise be structural or social impediments. Evidence from a diverse set of cases further suggest that because of nearly universal beliefs that women are comparatively non-violent and a-/less-political than men, many civilians view women rebels as most trustworthy and least threatening in areas ranging from recruitment and fundraising to outreach and welfare.[86]

---

[82] Ibid.

[83] Luisa Maria Dietrich Ortega, "Gendered Patterns of Mobilization and Recruitment for Political Violence, Experiences from Three Latin American Countries," in *Understanding Collective Political Violence*, ed. Yvan Guichaoua, Conflict, Inequality and Ethnicity (Palgrave Macmillan, 2012): 84–104; Swechchha Dahal, "Challenging the Boundaries: The Narratives of the Female Ex-Combatants in Nepal," in *Female Combatants in Conflict and Peace: Challenging Gender in Violence and Post-Conflict Reintegration*, ed. Seema Shekhawat (Palgrave Macmillan, 2015); Devorah Manekin and Reed M. Wood, "Framing the Narrative: Female Fighters, External Audience Attitudes, and Transnational Support for Armed Rebellions," *Journal of Conflict Resolution* 64, no. 9 (2020): 1638–65; Goldberg, "International Virtue Signaling."

[84] Loyle, "Rebel Justice during Armed Conflict," 109; Mampilly, *Rebel Rulers*; Arjona, *Rebelocracy*; Szekely, "Doing Well by Doing Good."

[85] Jennifer M. Larson and Janet I. Lewis, "Ethnic Networks," *American Journal of Political Science* 61, no. 2 (2017): 350–64.

[86] Viterna, *Women in War*; Natalia Herrera and Douglas Porch, "'Like Going to a Fiesta' – the Role of Female Fighters in Colombia's FARC-EP," *Small Wars & Insurgencies* 19, no. 4 (2008): 609–34; Dietrich Ortega, "Gendered Patterns of Mobilization and Recruitment for

Moreover, rebels often intend governance projects to help them overcome legacies of or complement their violent activities and to demonstrate that they are capable political groups.[87] By supplanting one legitimacy-building mechanism – governance – with another – women's visible involvement -, rebels might see women's participation in rebellion, generally, and governance, specifically, as a doubly fruitful avenue towards these ends. As one Syrian activist noted during the country's civil war, "Women are more dangerous than weapons. If you want to spread your ideology, the best way to do it is through women."[88]

These factors help explain demand-side rebel recruitment and deployment of women in rebel governance roles. But many women also seek out governance roles because they see opportunities for which they are well-suited, because participation in some areas of governance seems a 'natural' extension of their lives and work outside of conflict, because they want to expand or change existing efforts, or because they want to renegotiate rebellions' gendered dynamics through strategic activism. In fact, women's contributions to governance and to rebellion more broadly are very often 'ground-up' engagements initiated by women themselves.

Gilbert provides an instructive example through Syrian women's involvement in rebel governance. Women were largely initially excluded from local governance councils in rebel-held areas, but many were able to "institutionalize roles for women in local governance" including "significant roles in institutions that provided essential public goods and enforced laws for communities caught in the cross-fire" in what was primarily a grassroots effort.[89] Gilbert suggests that many women were interested in governance; that their pre- and during-war networking provided the organizational capacity needed to demand their inclusion; and that these efforts were most effective when rebel leadership was open to women's participation or could not enforce more conservative gender beliefs of hardliners in their ranks. And women's participation in this case was hard-won: though women relied heavily on civil society organizing to build a political position and negotiate entry into rebel spaces, the Syrian regime's prevention of emerging civil society organizations until 2011 meant that these women had to build political capacity "under violent conditions where deprivation and hardship were the norm."[90]

Political Violence, Experiences from Three Latin American Countries"; International Labour Organization, "IMU Recruits Migrant Workers," *AP Migration, ILO Regional Office for Asia and the Pacific* (2011), https://apmigration.ilo.org/news/imu-recruits-migrant-workers.

[87] Szekely, "Doing Well by Doing Good"; Loyle et al., "Revolt and Rule"; Heger and Jung, "Negotiating with Rebels."

[88] Quoted in Adam Heffez, "Using Women to Win in Syria," *Al-Monitor* (2013), 1, www.al-monitor.com/originals/2013/09/women-fighters-syria-rebels-regime.html.

[89] Victoria Gilbert, "Sister Citizens: Women in Syrian Rebel Governance," *Politics & Gender* 17, no. 4 (2021): 552–79.

[90] Ibid., 556.

It is not only why and when women participate in rebellion and in rebel governance that matters, but also how. Governance, as a (usually) set of several programs, is often administered by different parts of rebels' organizational structures. This varies significantly across groups, in part because of differing internal structures, and in some cases these institutions are administered through specific departments like health or education. Over 30 percent of rebellions also include associated women's wings whose primary focus is noncombatant work.[91] These wings concentrate and organize the skills, knowledge, and activities that women bring to rebellions' organizational structures. While some of these departments focus on support for military apparatuses, many women's wings engage in service provision and civilian oversight. They are often socially integrated with the population and assume responsibility as a link between rebels and the community. As the KWO case illustrates, rebellions that intend to engage with civilians may be especially likely to support these types of units. Women's wings also provide women a space to mobilize, exercise leadership and political capital, and create governance projects on their own accords, including in the face of resistance from rebel leadership.

The Communist Party of Nepal- Maoist (CPN-M), for example included a women's department under direct control of the Central Party that was created, according to Hisila Yami (Comrade Parvati), one of its former leaders, to "develop leadership qualities of women in all the three fronts, the Party, military and the united fronts" and to cultivate "leadership qualities right from home, which can later be tapped by the party to give political and ideological education" at the mass level.[92] Yami describes the women's department as "basically a policy making organization" that also offered study courses and classes to women; the CPN-M also included a "schooling department" with a "separate syllabus ... being prepared for women and oppressed nationality [sic]."[93]

Similarly, Hamas' Women's Action Department was involved in educational, cultural, women's, and political affairs.[94] Hamas established the women's wing alongside its newly created political organization in 1995. Recruiting educated, professional, and politically active women, the Women's Department focused on public relations and gendered politics and also helped the central party run kindergartens and organize workshops and educational trainings for the families

---

[91] Matfess and Loken, "Women's Wings in Rebel Organisations."

[92] Hilisa Yami, *People's War and Women's Liberation in Nepal* (Janadhwani, 2007): 96

[93] Ibid., 102.

[94] Islah Jad, "Islamist Women of Hamas: Between Feminism and Nationalism," *Inter-Asia Cultural Studies* 12, no. 2 (2011): 176.

of political prisoners.[95] Hamas women were reportedly involved in decision making, with female representatives in the central politburo.[96]

Women also participate widely in other political, cultural, and service-focused departments beyond all-women's units. For example, estimates suggest that women composed just under 40 percent of NMSP cadres in Myanmar but, though militarily-trained, most joined the organization's health and education departments.[97] As I discuss below, women further contribute to rebels' regulatory governance: for example, the NMSP's court system included female administrators, and many groups also incorporate women into judicial and policing units designed to enforce rebel rules among civilians.

Governance Expansion

The previous section demonstrates that how and where women participate in rebel groups can contribute to what governance looks like and help explain why armed organizations mobilize women for governance work and why women seek out these roles. These dynamics can also help us understand the gendered expansion of rebel governance projects: a larger organizational apparatus, the concentration of women's skills and networks, the peerless, gendered access women often have to some segments of civilian communities, and the potential cultivation of legitimacy and support among domestic and international populations due to women's involvement likely all contribute to the scope and scale of governance institutions.

Women's participation in governance can, firstly, expand rebels' civilian regulation and monitoring programs. This may be particularly true in communities where rebels' gender beliefs mandate social divisions between women and men, meaning that they may see men executing some types of rule enforcement as unacceptable gender-mixing. For example, in Yemen an all-female Houthi policing and intelligence force, the *Zaynabiyat*, carries out violent "morality policing" of women accused of traveling without a male relative, of prostitution or other "dishonorable" activities (often with little or no evidence), and of gender integration.[98] The unit polices Yemeni women through home raids, regulating women's dress and behavior in public, and abducting violators and women thought to be dissidents off of the street. Al-Hamdani suggests that

[95] Ibid.   [96] Ibid.

[97] Åshild Kolås, *Women, Peace and Security in Myanmar: Between Feminism and Ethnopolitics* (Routledge, 2019); Ashley South, *Mon Nationalism and Civil War in Burma: The Golden Sheldrake* (Routledge, 2013).

[98] Sama'a Al-Hamdani, "Understanding the Houthi Faction in Yemen," *Lawfare* (2019, 1), www.lawfaremedia.org/article/understanding-houthi-faction-yemen.

the *Zaynabiyat* "provides the only significant female representation" within the Houthi organization.[99]

Within the Allied Democratic Forces (ADF) in Uganda, there is similarly a "Police Officer for Women" and a woman in leadership who is reportedly in charge of both women's security and of women prisoners.[100] But this type of rules-based gendered governance is not limited to religious or gender-conservative rebellions. For example, within the CPN-M, the women's front, the All Nepal Women's Association (Revolutionary) (ANWA-R), supported gender equality in society and implemented related rules at the community level. The ANWA-R was responsible for enforcing anti-domestic violence rules, banning the practice of menstruating women sleeping in cowsheds, and preventing polygamy and child marriages.[101]

On, it seems, a larger scale, women participate as executors of service provision programs and administrative roles. Take, for example, the Eritrean People's Liberation Front (EPLF), which emerged in the 1970s during the war for Eritrea's independence from Ethiopia. The organization invested heavily in governance, including maintaining utilities and roads, providing healthcare through hospitals and mobile medical teams, offering educational, literacy, and occupational training programs, instituting educational programs aimed at expanding women's rights, altering local and land inheritance and marriage laws, establishing a justice system, and installing civilian-led People's Assemblies.[102] This ambitious agenda required the EPLF to recruit widely and the group viewed the total mobilization of society as critical to achieving their material objectives. But the organization also recruited women, specifically, as part of their ideological project of women's liberation.[103] The EPLF actively mobilized women into frontline roles, but women also contributed significantly to and helped grow these governance programs. Thomas and Bond conclude that EPLF women "served as intermediaries between the armed front and the population," occupying positions across governance programs and engaging in outreach.[104] Eritrean women had little access to formal education or training before the independence war, and the EPLF specifically recruited and trained women in the skills required to administer to the civilian population. For example, women were first integrated in EPLF educational structures as students and then as teachers. The EPLF also trained women

---

[99] Ibid., 1.

[100] Congo Research Group, *Inside the ADF Rebellion: A Glimpse into the Life and Operations of a Secretive Jihadi Armed Group* (2018). It is not clear if the report is referring to the same woman in both roles or different women.

[101] Seira Tamang, "The Politics of Conflict and Difference or the Difference of Conflict in Politics: The Women's Movement in Nepal," *Feminist Review* 91, no. 1 (2009): 61–80.

[102] Stewart, *Governing for Revolution.*   [103] Ibid.

[104] Thomas and Bond, "Women's Participation in Violent Political Organizations," 502.

to be doctors, working in the mobile health clinics to expand them to hard-to-reach communities.[105] Relying on reports from a former fighter, Bernal suggests that many women who became frontline fighters "were, in fact, assigned to combat duty because they lacked specialized skills that could contribute significantly to support activities."[106]

Finally, there is some preliminary evidence that women's roles within rebel governance might model groups' gender beliefs, and therefore their ultimate view of gender order in society, to the civilian population. Rebels' desire to enforce or reform existing gender order among civilians can be a central part of rebel's ideological governance campaigns (see Section 5 for a discussion about these dynamics).[107] Sovereignty is not only about tactical power, but also about the fantasy of an ideal citizenry. Identifying and enforcing a specific, gendered "binary arrangement of order verses anarchy" is a quintessential state function.[108] Where and how women are part of rebel governance, then, may be an important vehicle for conveying this articulation of gendered order to and expanding its reach across civilians. For example, Matfess demonstrates how some rebellions' internal marriage regulations "extend beyond the group's ranks to affect civilians' marriage practices and eligibility."[109]

This is a speculative theoretical extension: we cannot know what impact rebels' gendered beliefs might have on civilians without information from civilians themselves about their perceptions. But consider the LTTE. The organization saw expanding women's roles as a key part of their ideology of Tamil nationalism and mobilized this as a central part of socio-political reform.[110] To this end, the group adopted a gender-inclusive regime incorporating women into the group despite rigid, conservative gender norms in their national community. These roles mirrored the gender reform that the LTTE attempted in Tamil society, and it elicited significant pushback from many civilians who saw it, correctly, as a manifestation of the group's broader gender-reform agenda.[111] While this example concerns women combatants, it lays theoretical groundwork to consider that women's involvement in other roles, like governance, might help expand and implement not only tangible projects but also rebels' ideological gendered agendas among the civilian population.

---

[105] Victoria Bernal, "From Warriors to Wives: Contradictions of Liberation and Development in Eritrea," *Northeast African Studies* 8, no. 3 (2001): 129–54.

[106] Ibid., 134.   [107] Stewart, *Governing for Revolution*.

[108] Cynthia Weber, *Queer International Relations: Sovereignty, Sexuality and the Will to Knowledge*, Oxford Studies in Gender and International Relations (Oxford University Press, 2016): 4–5.

[109] Matfess, "In Love and at War," 17.

[110] Terpstra and Frerks, "Rebel Governance and Legitimacy."   [111] Ibid.

Governance Development

In many rebellions women do not only administer or make more expansive existing programs, they also orchestrate new governance efforts. Women construct institutions that we would likely not observe in their absence. These are often focused on women's political engagement, empowerment, and education; on service provision and welfare for civilians; and on children. This is possible, at least in part, because women compose significant proportions of the decision-making leadership in many rebellions. Available data suggests that nearly 40 percent of rebel groups include women in noncombatant leadership roles, for example within congresses, councils, other internal legislative or administrative bodies, women's wings, and other departments.[112] And these governance priorities align with research on women's leadership in other policy-making roles that concludes that *who* is provisioning public goods affects what those goods are: evidence from village-level and national-level studies find that women are often more involved in issues related to women's rights and children, and leaders "invest more in infrastructure that is directly relevant to the needs of their own genders."[113] In India, for example, women village leaders were more likely than men to invest in issues raised as concerns by women, such as a lack of drinking water, which women were in charge of collecting.[114] This is arguably because women public goods provisioners may often have a stronger sense of the issues, in and out of wartime, most pressing for other women in their communities.

Above, I discussed Gilbert's research on women who participated in Syrian rebels' governance efforts. In this case, women fought – successfully – to establish new institutions, including "Women's Offices or Offices for the Support of Women – institutions that were part of the local council, run by women, and were intended to both promote the involvement of women in local councils and address the needs of local women" during the war.[115] They focused on education and professional training and advocated for women's participation in politics.[116] Syrian groups' control of territory and programs fluctuated as the war pushed civilians into constantly contested areas and new armed group alliances formed and failed, meaning that perhaps governance programs were also in flux. But such programmic development is not unique to groups where constant change may create openings for innovation – women build new governance efforts in highly centralized groups as well.

---

[112] Loken and Matfess, "Introducing the Women's Activities in Armed Rebellion (WAAR) Project, 1946–2015."

[113] Raghabendra Chattopadhyay and Esther Duflo, "Women as Policy Makers: Evidence from a Randomized Policy Experiment in India," *Econometrica* 72, no. 5 (2004): 1409–43.

[114] Ibid.   [115] Gilbert, "Sister Citizens," 555.   [116] Ibid.

The African National Congress (ANC) in South Africa is an exemplar. The Women's Section of the ANC was reportedly, to the chagrin of some of its members, "the movement's social worker" for the first decade of its operations while the organization was in exile.[117] ANC leadership did not initially advance a clear plan for the Women's Section but relied on it for civilian outreach. But women within the group saw the Women's Section as making "women's activism possible" and so they took their roles very seriously, building new and sizeable programs aimed at supporting ANC members, their families, and their supporters.[118] This included establishing and staffing schools, creating childcare facilities, and processing and distributing food and donated goods. The Women's Section explicitly stressed the maternal aspects of their governance work and their roles as proverbial mothers of the movement. Hassim writes,

> Although the ANC had a policy of keeping families together whenever possible, many children were separated from their parents, and members of the ANC Women's Section acted as surrogate mothers – an effort to make the nurseries 'a home and not an institution.' Mavis Nhlapo, administrative secretary for the Women's Section in the early 1980s, said that 'the maternal instinct of protection certainly drove the Women's Section.' An MK [ANC armed wing] cadre noted that 'I didn't have to choose between motherhood and politics because the Women's Section made it possible for me to do both. I knew I could leave my child in good hands.' This was a minority view, though: most women in the movement were very unhappy about being separated from their children.[119]

The ANC Women's Section demonstrates how women, and women working in women's wings, specifically, create new governance programs and shape the content of existing work. Another example in this vein comes from the Farabundo Martí Liberation People's Forces (FPL) in El Salvador, a group that ultimately joined with other organizations to form the FMLN. The FPL operated individual fronts and while there was centralized leadership, militants working in these fronts established and administered programs with some independence. This included individuals and groups of FPL women who shaped practices of civilian engagement. In one case, FPL women helped established a council government run by civilians and organized with the FPL's women's wing, the Association of Salvadoran Women (AMES).[120] The AMES, which was "composed of combatants, peasants, and militants in exile, [...] collectivized food production, shaped the

---

[117] Shireen Hassim, *Women's Organizations and Democracy in South Africa: Contesting Authority* (University of Wisconsin Press, 2006): 88.

[118] Ibid.   [119] Ibid., 89.

[120] Diana Sierra Becerra, *Insurgent Butterflies: Gender and Revolution in El Salvador, 1965–2015* (Ph.D. dissertation, University of Michigan, 2017).

agenda of health clinics to address gynecological health [...] created childcare centers that enabled the political participation of women and taught children anti-sexist values, [... and] intervened in domestic disputes, denouncing men who opposed the political participation of their wives and daughters."[121]

Not all women's wings help develop new governance programs, and women's participation in governance is not a sufficient condition for projects that tend specifically to women civilians or specific issues. The desire to advance such programming, the political capital and capacity to do so, the working relationships between broader rebel leadership and women partici-pating in governance, the degree of relative autonomy enjoyed by women's wings, and the internal gender dynamics of rebel groups all likely contribute to when and how women develop and execute new governance programs. In Syria, women succeeded in these projects despite exclusion in part because they had the political and organizational capacity to overcome barriers to entry.[122] In the FPL case, the AMES benefited from rebel leadership backing their efforts to mobilize women and spread FPL ideology and rules within the civilian population.[123]

Multi-layered Governance

The three dynamics that I have discussed thus far are focused internally on some-what formal rebel programming and on the contributions of women members. But examining women's contributions to rebellion, and governance specifically, also requires us to re-think the relationships between rebel groups and their communities and the presumed top-down flow of governance. There exist idiosyncratic, gray-area networks between rebel, state, and civilian governance systems that necessarily arise during civil wars. And across many contexts, women compose the core of these networks that do not always fall cleanly into either rebel governance or civilian self-help categories as traditionally described. Here, I draw on and extend Kasfir, Frerks, and Terpstra's notion of 'multi-layered governance' – the reality of multiple, diverse armed groups governing civilians during some civil wars – to explain how civilian-led and civilian-rebel hybrid governance, and women as primary actors of said governance, adds more empirical and analytic layers to understanding these practices.[124] While this aspect of governance may not speak directly to the empirical associations identified in the previous section, it is a related, important part of understanding gendered governance.

---

[121] Ibid., 149 and 4.   [122] Gilbert, "Sister Citizens."

[123] Sierra Becerra, "Insurgent Butterflies."

[124] Nelson Kasfir, Georg Frerks, and Niels Terpstra, "Introduction Armed Groups and Multi-layered Governance," *Civil Wars*, 19, no. 3 (2017): 257–78.

Kasfir, Freks, and Terpstra introduce the concept of 'multi-layered governance' to capture the complexity of environments where state forces, rebel
groups, and other armed actors like self-defense forces or vigilantes administer
governance at different levels.[125] But these actors – rebel groups, in the scope of
this Element – also engage in governance with and alongside community
members, working in tandem or in the same areas to provision for and police
civilian populations. As the symbolic and material centers of community life in
most societies, it is often women who contribute most extensively to this kind of
governance. Sometimes this includes the development of new programs. This is
especially true in cases, like the aforementioned KNU, where rebellions emerge
from a population largely supportive of their objectives. Scholars often concep-
tualize rebellions in this category as "people's wars," or "parastate conflicts"
wherein much of society is involved to some degree in contentious efforts
against the state.

Take, for example, food provisioning. In conflicts that could arguably be
classified as "people's wars," including in Myanmar, Angola, Cambodia,
and the Philippines, community women engaged in food provisioning for
both armed groups and civilians in war-affected areas.[126] Hedström and
colleagues discuss this, in the Myanmar context, as the 'revolutionary
household' from which women maintain and sustain life and rebellion
outside of or in weak association with military institutions.[127] In Uganda,
the National Resistance Army/Movement (NRA/M) mobilized collective
farms where women organized other women, and men, to grow crops to be
distributed to the group and the community, but women were solely
responsible for collecting food from the fields because men "could be
shot dead on sight."[128]

There is often also collaboration between women outside the armed group
structure and those within it. The aforementioned EPLF case is illustrative here;
the EPLF instated a 15 percent quota for women's representation in the People's
Assemblies, civilian-led structures that governed areas under the rebel groups'
control in ways consistent with their ideals.[129] The NRA/M provides another
useful example. In the group's early years the NRA/M excluded women from
rebel membership but by the end of its first year had adopted a strategy wherein
women were not permitted to formally join but still participated in active

---

[125] Ibid.   [126] Hedström, "Militarized Social Reproduction."

[127] Jenny Hedström, Hilary Oliva Faxon, Zin Mar Phyo et al., "Forced Fallow Fields: Making
Meaningful Life in the Myanmar Spring Revolution," *Civil Wars* (2023): 1–25. https://doi.org/
10.1080/13698249.2023.2240620.

[128] Beatrice Mugambe, *Women's Roles in Armed Conflict and Their Marginalisation* (Organization
for Social Science Research in Eastern and Southern Africa, 2000): 10.

[129] Stewart, *Governing for Revolution.*

noncombatant service.[130] Women later began joining the army and participating in combat, including holding leadership roles and fighting as part of a women's unit.[131] At the same time, the NRA/M organized governance structures for civilian participation in democratic politics (including civilian-led elections), village committees to oversee local issues, and clandestine 'resistance committees' to grow and distribute food, recruit, and provide intelligence.[132] Women participated widely in these civilian-led governance structures, liaising and working with women more formally involved in the organization.[133] Civilian women and those who were part of the NRA/M were also involved in providing healthcare to the population, including as traditional birth attendants or nurses; NRA/M women were also involved in mass food provisioning.[134]

Another important factor in multi-layered governance is the relationships between civil society organizations and rebel groups. In many conflicts, women's groups founded as independent organizations become associated with, but not entirely tied to, armed groups while working in tandem towards their shared goals. This includes rebels' governance objectives. For example, in the Kashmir region the Dukhtaran-e-Millat (DeM) was created and operated as a women's Islamist political organization though it was affiliated with rebel groups. Women of the DeM engaged in policing as part of their ideological salience with and advocacy for Islamist rebels' causes, including preventing women from joining military training.[135] The group, for example, enforced strict gender segregation and the *burqa* for women in public, targeting "locations that are supposedly the hubs of 'immoral' activities, such as cafes, restaurants, liquor shops, hotels, internet cafes, and even gift shops."[136] Eventually the DeM worked "specifically with separatist and hard-line militant groups like the Lashkar-e-Jhangvi (LeJ) [and Jamaat-i-Islami] to enforce the Islamic code of conduct in the Kashmir Valley."[137] The organization also operated religious schools for women and girls.

It is therefore not enough in many conflicts to consider only women's participation as members of rebel organizations, we must take seriously the governance work that civilians take on in the absence of an administrative or protective state. Though this labor is sometimes performed in coordination with or support for

---

[130] Aili Mari Tripp, *Women & Politics in Uganda* (University of Wisconsin Press, 2000); Elizabeth L. Brannon, "Celebrated and Sidelined: How Women's Roles in the National Resistance Army Shaped Post-Conflict Gender Politics," *Civil Wars* (2023): 1–24. https://doi.org/10.1080/13698249.2023.2230812.

[131] Brannon, "Celebrated and Sidelined."

[132] Nelson Kasfir, "Guerrillas and Civilian Participation: The National Resistance Army in Uganda, 1981–86," *The Journal of Modern African Studies* 43, no. 2 (2005): 271–96.

[133] Mugambe, "Women's Roles in Armed Conflict and Their Marginalisation."   [134] Ibid.

[135] Swati Parashar, "Gender, Jihad, and Jingoism: Women as Perpetrators, Planners, and Patrons of Militancy in Kashmir," *Studies in Conflict & Terrorism* 34, no. 4 (2011): 295–317.

[136] Ibid., 303.   [137] Ibid., 303–4.

rebellions, in other cases civilians work in the interests of broader political movements and ideological objectives. Moreover, to understand the gendered contours of rebel governance is to recognize multi-layered governances and their importance for rebels' trajectories. While we do not have data that captures these relationships at a cross-conflict or comparative level, the empirical realities described here suggest that these can be influential and gendered relationships.

Mechanisms at Work

In Section 1, I discussed briefly some of the key factors that underly trends in rebel governance: desire for domestic and international legitimacy, strong administrative and human capacities, centralized organizational structures, and the need to demonstrate authority, create order, and mandate civilian compliance. Insights from the gendered dynamics of rebel governance suggest that because women's involvement can shape the content and execution of these efforts and expand and develop both service provision and regulatory programs, this may help rebel groups engender legitimacy, establish authority, and enable more extensive civilian monitoring. These factors may help explain positive associations between women's noncombatant involvement and governance institutions at the cross-conflict level.

But rebels with more transformational agendas may also simply need more significant human resources to operate expansive programs, making their governance institutions and women's recruitment symptoms of the same cause: their material needs. It is probable that these relationships result not only from women's contributions but also from rebels' organizational and structural conditions. Still, research does suggest key differences in the organizational characteristics related to governance provision and those related to women's involvement. Communist ideologies appear not significantly associated with rebel governance but have a very significant, positive relationship with women's recruitment.[138] Groups with secessionist aims appear the most likely to provide services to civilians, but secessionist aims may have a significantly negative effect on women's participation.[139] It is therefore likely that the relationships between women's noncombatant involvement and rebels' implementation of governance programs cannot be entirely explained by other correlating factors. There is no good way to disentangle these complex relationships in service of one-way causal

---

[138] Stewart, "Civil War as State-Making"; Reed M. Wood and Jakana L. Thomas, "Women on the Frontline: Rebel Group Ideology and Women's Participation in Violent Rebellion," *Journal of Peace Research* 54, no. 1 (2017): 31–46. This work looks specifically at women in combat.

[139] Stewart, "Civil War as State-Making"; Thomas and Bond, "Women's Participation in Violent Political Organizations."

identification. Nor is it theoretically appropriate to do so – gendered governance relationships are complex and occur from multiple directions.

It is clear, however, that rebels' recruitment practices, the scope, scale, and development of governance programs, and rebel engagement with civilians are gendered in consequential ways. In this section, I described how gender matters for analyzing and understanding four dynamics of rebel governance. How do these dynamics play out within and across rebellions? In the next section, I explore these dynamics in three diverse organizations to demonstrate the utility of this framework and the importance of women's participation for rebel governance outcomes. This detailed case study evidence explicates gendered governance relationships and the contributions that women make to rebels' non-fighting campaigns. Moreover, it contextualizes and offers explanations for the patterns identified at the cross-conflict level in Section 2.

4 Dynamics of Gendered Governance in Three Rebellions

How do dynamics of gendered governance manifest during civil wars? How is women's noncombatant participation related to governance institutions? In Section 3, I identify four individual but interrelated gendered dynamics of rebel governance that illuminate these practices: recruitment and internal organization, governance expansion, governance development, and multi-layered governance. In this section, I leverage three diverse cases of rebel governance during civil wars to explore the context, importance, and implications of these relationships.

The three cases that I focus on are IS (2013–2019/present),[140] Fretilin (1974–1999), and the Provisional IRA and related militant republican groups (1969–1998).[141] I choose these cases to account for key structural and socio-cultural differences that studies suggest are important for the scope of rebel governance practices and for the level and type of women's participation in armed groups. These include rebel territorial control, which can provide groups greater incentives and resources to provide governance and appears associated with recruiting women;[142] social transformation as an ideological and military objective, as rebel governance programs are generally most expansive in groups with the most transformational goals and these institutions

---

[140] Coalition forces retook IS' last significantly held territory in Syria in 2019, but the group persists today as a more loosely affiliated organization.

[141] The organization formally ended its armed campaign in 2005 but its political wing, Sinn Féin, signed the Good Friday accords in 1998 after the Provisional IRA declared a ceasefire in 1997.

[142] Arjona, Kasfir, and Mampilly, *Rebel Governance in Civil War*; Victor Asal and Amira Jadoon, "When Women Fight: Unemployment, Territorial Control and the Prevalence of Female Combatants in Insurgent Organizations," *Dynamics of Asymmetric Conflict* 13, no. 3 (2020): 258–81.

can include new inclusive or exclusive gender rules;[143] and, relatedly, prevailing internal and external gender norms, which may affect rebels' willingness to recruit women into specific roles or women's motivations to join.[144] Moreover, each case illustrates or contextualizes several of the gendered governance dynamics that ground this Element's framework.

First, IS controlled significant territory in two states and advanced an extremely transformational agenda that involved a revolution of the state structure and of gender rules in society. The group included comparatively few women in most parts of its organization. Still, IS' recruitment of women into noncombatant and governance roles and women's expansion of existing IS programs helps us better understand the group's administration and civilian management practices.

Next, during Fretilin's anti-colonial war against Indonesia the group and their territories moved and changed frequently as military incursions targeted the rebellion. Fretilin aspired to less transformational goals than IS but still aimed to restructure social orders like gender and class as a central part of their ideology. They included women at most levels of their operations, though not evenly. Here, the dynamics of women's recruitment and their participation in both program expansion and development are central to explaining the trajectory of the rebellion's governance projects.

Finally, the Provisional IRA weakly controlled territory only at the neighborhood or street level and sought primarily to restructure the government and its policies. The Provisional IRA and their political affiliates included women in moderate numbers and highly visible positions in all roles. Women's participation as governance project developers is essential to explaining the groups' programs in this case, as is the critical role that multi-layered governance involving women-centered civilian networks played in sustaining these institutions and the broader movement.

In sum, these cases demonstrate the utility of a gendered approach for understanding rebel governance across groups of different ideologies, aims, structures, resources, and broader levels of women's engagement. Moreover, these cases help illustrate why and how rebellions recruit women for and women take on these projects as well as how women's contributions influence the practice, expansion, and development of governance.

Islamic State

Islamic State is, in many ways, representative of a wide range of rebellions. An estimated 35 percent of rebellions control domestic territory, incentivizing and

---

[143] Stewart, *Governing for Revolution*.

[144] Reed M. Wood, *Female Fighters: Why Rebel Groups Recruit Women for War* (Columbia University Press, 2019).

providing opportunities for governance programs.[145] But IS uniquely achieved extensive territorial control, eventually becoming "the most expansive case of jihadist governance in history."[146] As part of this project, IS introduced a new sociopolitical regime into parts of Iraq and Syria and instituted unusually strict oversight of the civilian population. This regime relied in large part on a total reconfiguration of the gendered relations of civilian life and on explicit restrictions imposed on women, but this agenda also required women's participation in governance to enact such a transformative vision. This case illustrates how rebellions' gendered recruitment and internal organizational patterns shape their governance agendas and explicates the importance of women's contributions to governance expansion, in both regulatory and provision-based institutions.

Background

IS originated as al-Qaeda in Iraq during Iraq's civil war in the mid-2000s. Following internal leadership splits within the broad al-Qaeda network, AQI broke away and rebranded as IS, shifting focus from expelling the United States from Iraq and toward the establishment of an "Islamic State" modeled on the earliest forms of Islamic governance.[147] Capitalizing on the outbreak of Syria's civil war in 2011 and governmental weakness in Iraq, IS swept through the two countries seizing territory. By 2013, the organization had established courts in Syria and was providing services to civilians.[148] In mid-2014, IS declared a 'caliphate' – a politico-religious "state" modeled on the Prophet Mohammed's Islamic governance structure – with Mosul, Iraq as its capital. Between 2014 and 2017 the organization established control of up to half of Syrian territory and one third of Iraq, governing 10 million people.[149] Eventually, counterinsurgency reduced IS territory to negligible areas of control in these countries.

IS' governance programs were multi-purpose: they were a practical means of establishing a borderless caliphate; a method of generating resources, building legitimacy, earning civilian support, and mandating civilian compliance; and a propagandistic tool aimed at both local and international audiences.[150]

---

[145] Megan A. Stewart and Yu-Ming Liou, "Do Good Borders Make Good Rebels? Territorial Control and Civilian Casualties," *The Journal of Politics* 79, no. 1 (2017): 284–301.

[146] Joana Cook, "Women in Jihadist Practices of Governance: The Case of Al-Qaeda and ISIS," in *The Rule Is for None but Allah: Islamist Approaches to Governance*, ed. Joana Cook and Shiraz Maher (Hurst, 2023): 205.

[147] Mara Redlich Revkin and Ariel I. Ahram, "Perspectives on the Rebel Social Contract: Exit, Voice, and Loyalty in the Islamic State in Iraq and Syria," *World Development* 132 (2020): 1–9.

[148] Ibid.   [149] Cook, "Women in Jihadist Practices of Governance."

[150] Revkin, "Competitive Governance and Displacement Decisions under Rebel Rule" *Journal of Conflict Resolution* 65, no. 1 (2021): 46–80; Revkin, "What Explains Taxation by Resource-Rich Rebels?"; Cook, "Women in Jihadist Practices of Governance."

IS governed through what Revkin and Ahram identify as a "rebel social contract," wherein the group "must offer a set of protections and benefits to the population in expectation of receiving support" and civilians "must accept, either voluntarily or involuntarily, the rebel offer."[151] This social contract is most evidently clear through the "constitution-like 'charters of the city' (*wathīqa al-madīnah*)" that IS published first in Mosul and Raqqa, Syria, and then later throughout the entire "caliphate."[152] These charters laid out the tangible services IS offered, including, for example, civilian rights under the judicial system and public goods provisions, but also articulated the ideological contract to which IS expected civilians' compliance. These "duties of adherence" to IS' religious interpretations centered in part on a restrictive gender regime at the heart of the group leadership's desired sociopolitical project. For example, the later *Wathīqa al-Madīnah* mandates, "To the virtuous and dignified women .... Dress decently and in loose tunics and robes .... Do not leave the house except out of necessity."[153] IS enforced these gendered charters and other directives through religious rulings.[154]

Gendered Governance

IS' "social contract" in Syria and Iraq mandated a system of gender segregation and regulation as a core manifestation of the rebellion's ideology. And while IS' gendered governance of civilians is well documented through its system of dress, marriage, and movement restrictions for women living under rebel control,[155] the organization's incorporation of women as part of this governance structure demonstrates how women's participation helped the group build its administration and promote its ideology within its territories.

While IS governed millions of women civilians who remained in their communities after the group took power, the organization also widely recruited women, locally and internationally, to work in IS administration, recruit, fundraise, and proselytize their lives as wives and mothers in IS families.[156] The organization did not recruit women into front-line roles, though a handful of

---

[151] Revkin and Ahram, "Perspectives on the Rebel Social Contract," 2.   [152] Ibid.
[153] Islamic State (2016). "Charter of the City" (*Wathiqat al-Madinah*), quoted in Beatrice De Graaf and Ahmet S. Yayla, *Policing as Rebel Governance: The Islamic State Police* (Program on Extremism, 2021).
[154] Devorah Margolin and Charlie Winter, *Women in the Islamic State: Victimization, Support, Collaboration, and Acquiescence* (Program on Extremism, 2021).
[155] Islamic State, "The Ruling of Hijrah Women without a Guardian," (Jihadology, 2015); Margolin and Winter, *Women in the Islamic State.*
[156] Meredith Loken and Anna Zelenz, "Explaining Extremism: Western Women in Daesh," *European Journal of International Security* 3, no. 1 (2018): 45–68; Gina Vale, *Women in Islamic State: From Caliphate to Camps* (ICCT Policy Brief, 2019); Cook, "Women in Jihadist Practices of Governance."

women appeared to take up arms in the group's final territorial days. But IS' enforcement of gender segregation and relegation of women to private life paradoxically required women participating in the group's public governance to execute this transformation of society. Islamic State leaders believed that men could not appropriately enforce such rules and norms. They therefore recruited women directly into their governance structures to expand both their civilian compliance and service provision programs in line with their broader ideological objectives. Women also joined because they saw these roles as an opportunity to escape the group's restrictive rules or, in other cases, because they wanted to participate in building IS' ideological and tangible future. Women's specific positions and public activities within IS' governance system represented and, arguably, aimed to legitimize, the group's authority within its territories and beyond.[157]

One primary way that women participated in IS governance was through the Department of Religious Compliance, the *hisba* department. These offices enforced the religious obligation to 'commanding right and forbidding wrong' through policing and surveillance of those living within areas under IS control. *Hisba* is, broadly, Islamic doctrines concerning community morals and behavior, including gendered ones, though there is significant variation in what different religious communities consider 'wrongdoing.' *Hisba* departments for IS were therefore public morality policing and enforcement of the religious rules that composed their 'social contract' with the public. A network of *hisba* departments existed at the provisional level in IS-held territory; within them, *hisba* offices existed at the district level and each operated field squads of enforcers, localizing the governance of the ruling party's ideological ideas.[158]

These departments included women's *hisba* offices to enforce the rebel group's rules concerning women.[159] In service to IS' principles and the expansion of its reach over the civilian population, *hisba* women – and others participating in IS' governance structure – were permitted to take on leadership roles that were in some ways at odds with IS' view of gender and women in society. As Moaveni contends, *hisba* brigades "reflected, in various institutional forms, the growing and widening place of women in administrative, educational, health, recruitment,

---

[157] Many women civilians living in territory where IS took control were also forced into administrative roles. Those working for the government or in the education system similarly had few choices other than to continue working for the "state" once IS gained control.

[158] Asaad Almohammad and Clemens Holzgruber, *Moral Dominance: Policing Minds, Spirits, Bodies, and Markets* (Program on Extremism, 2021).

[159] Men enforce morality rules concerning women in many other organizations with similar gendered segregation.

and propaganda wings of the Islamic State," often necessitated by the strict gender rules that grounded IS' ideology and governance model.[160]

Some women shared this sociopolitical vision and wanted to be part of IS' proto-state system. Other women report joining *hisba* brigades because it was one of the only activities that allowed them opportunities outside the home or to work.[161] After attending compulsory religious courses and weapons training, women of the *hisba*, often armed, patrolled the streets in vans or on foot, monitoring civilian women and arresting or confronting those violating religious codes in their dress or behavior.[162] They enforced IS rules violently, whipping and beating women or cutting their fingers over minor infractions, such as wearing makeup or overly tight *abayas*.[163] Women of the *hisba* were also responsible for disbursing other female IS members' salaries, transporting new female arrivals into IS-held territories, inspecting stores selling to and providing services for women, patrolling women's institutes and schools, and accompanying armed squads to carry out raids and examine captured women.[164]

One women's *hisba* unit, the al-Khansaa Brigade, published a 'manifesto' in 2015 that Winter describes as "a piece of propaganda aimed at busting myths and recruiting supporters."[165] The document, circulated online among Arabic-speaking networks, outlines gendered governance rules largely centered on women remaining veiled and at home. It also includes conditions under which women are permitted to leave the house, including when women nurses, doctors, and teachers are working in accordance with IS rules. The al-Khansaa Brigade lauded these regulations as a "hallowed existence" wherein women were "fulfilling their fundamental roles" as ordained by God.[166] The group encouraged women to appreciate and accept IS' gendered rules, concluding that such governance brings women, and all people, in line with IS' ideology and Qur'anic decrees. They contend, "When the Islamic State fully undertook administration of the land, the people regained their rights, none more so than women."[167]

[160] Azadeh Moaveni, *Guest House for Young Widows: Among the Women of ISIS* (Random House, 2019), 173.
[161] Ibid.
[162] Vale, "Defying Rules: Defying Gender?"; Islamic State, "Women's Dawa in the Islamic State: Internal Files," Aymenn Jawad Al-Tamimi, https://aymennjawad.org/2020/04/women-dawa-in-the-islamic-state-internal-files; Islamic State, "On Movement of Women and the Garages: Raqqa Province," Aymenn Jawad Al-Tamimi, "Archive of Islamic State Administrative Documents," (2015), www.aymennjawad.org/2015/01/archive-of-islamic-state-administrative-documents.
[163] Cook, "Women in Jihadist Practices of Governance," 224.
[164] Almohammad and Holzgruber, *Moral Dominance*.
[165] Islamic State, "Women of the Islamic State: A Manifesto on Women by the Al-Khansaa Brigade," trans. Charlie Winter (Quilliam Foundation, 2015): 6.
[166] Ibid., 12–18.   [167] Ibid., 29.

But women were not only responsible for civilian management aspects of governance; they were also critical to the expansion and embeddedness of many service programs among the civilian populations. For example, women were responsible for educating girls under IS' regime; unlike some jihadist organizations, IS viewed girls' basic – segregated – education as necessary for fulfilling their roles within the "caliphate." IS leaders believed that women could not raise and educate future generations "if she is illiterate and ignorant."[168] Educated women, therefore, established and ran educational institutes and worked in schools that taught girls Islamic history and religion, languages, geography, and other approved subjects. These activities "were at the heart of [IS'] community outreach efforts; after all, they enabled it to work to entrench the ideological basis for its system of control."[169]

Dr. Iman Mustafa al-Bagha, a prominent Syrian Islamic scholar and professor of Islamic law, joined IS and worked in the Fatwa Issuing and Research Department (*Diwan al-Iftaa' wa al-Buhuth*).[170] Identified by Moaveni as the "most prominent and influential female ideologue" within IS, al-Bagha viewed the organization as implementers of her pre-existing beliefs about Islamic law and so she joined the group to participate in their caliphate-building aspirations.[171]

al-Bagha ran a religious education center for women in Raqqa, the *Dhat al-Nataqain* institute, which included a staff of at least six female lecturers teaching approximately 350 students.[172] IS' Da'wa and Mosques Department (*Diwan al-Da'wa wa al-Masajid*), which oversaw these educational institutes, praised al-Bagha as a model of women's leadership within IS and "service of jihad in the path of God."[173] Still, IS leadership strictly controlled al-Bagha and others' curriculum: eventually, they reportedly took issue with some of her religious interpretations, beliefs, and teachings and closed her institute.[174] But al-Bagha exemplifies the role of educated women, many of whom were educated in Saudi Arabia, who taught women and girls living under IS rule. One woman, an al-Khansaa Brigade member, recalls being extraordinarily drawn to these women and their deeply learned teachings on Islam. Through this education, she says that she "found herself attracted to the idea of a real Islamic state."[175]

---

[168] Ibid., 18.   [169] Margolin and Winter, *Women in the Islamic State,* 32.

[170] Aymenn Jawad Al-Tamimi, "The Archivist: Stories of the Mujahideen: Unseen Islamic State Biographies of Outstanding Members," (2016), https://aymennjawad.org/19132/the-archivist-stories-of-the-mujahideen-unseen.

[171] Moaveni, *Guest House for Young Widows.*

[172] Aymenn Jawad Al-Tamimi, "Islamic State Internal Files on Dr. Imaan Mustafa al-Bagha," (2020), https://aymennjawad.org/2020/05/islamic-state-internal-files-on-dr-imaan-mustafa.

[173] Al-Tamimi, "The Archivist."

[174] Al-Tamimi, "Islamic State Internal Files on Dr. Imaan Mustafa al-Bagha."

[175] Moaveni, *Guest House for Young Widows,* 175.

Women in IS were also partially responsible for expanding and sustaining a unique type of service provision: housing for women and girls (and their children) who, for an array of reasons, were not living with their husbands. This included single, foreign women who had traveled to Syria or Iraq to join the organization, women who had joined with their husbands and who were waiting for them while they underwent military training, and widows whose husbands had been killed in combat and who would, eventually, remarry.[176] Reportedly "every town or city controlled by [IS] had one or several of these guest houses" where women slept several people to each room and that were managed by strict, female "house wardens."[177] Some of the wardens were the wives and daughters of powerful IS leaders – for example, the daughter of the IS Emir of Raqqa ran one such home. Women who stayed in this housing report cramped, boring, strict, neglected, and sometimes violent quarters awash with suspicion.[178] But this housing scheme, governed and maintained by IS women, was a cornerstone of IS' broader marriage and family system that underpinned its vision of the caliphate and scaffolded its operations.

Finally, outside of formal governance structures, women had a central role in representing and justifying IS' ideology and gendered governance through the rebellion's propaganda operations. For example, IS' official English-language publications included sections ostensibly written by women for female audiences. These articles discuss the benefits of IS' gender regime for women and encourage Muslims around the world to come and live under the 'caliphate.'[179] This includes highlighting the roles women took on within and under IS governance, largely a domestic, segregated life but with participation in IS administration as Islamic jurisprudence experts, doctors, *hisba* members, and engineers.[180] Moreover, these articles emphasize the 'caliphate' as a reasonable alternative for women and their families to the existing state system; they stress IS' strong administrative governance and service provision, for example, as well as the healthcare, education, food aid, and charitable giving for women.[181]

The gender rules integral to IS' governance were not wholly uncontested. Many IS women, even those who enthusiastically joined the organization, found the group's gender order stifling and misaligned with their practices of Islam.[182] Local Iraqi, Syrian, and Kurdish women resisted as well, providing information to anti-IS coalition forces, refusing to comply fully with attire

---

[176] Ibid.   [177] Ibid, 251.   [178] Ibid.
[179] See, for example, Dabiq, "From the Battles of Al-Ahzāb to the War of Coalitions," Issue 11 (2015).
[180] Cook, "Women in Jihadist Practices of Governance."
[181] Dabiq, "Just Terror," Issue 12 (2015); Cook, "Women in Jihadist Practices of Governance."
[182] Moaveni, *Guest House for Young Widows*.

requirements, and publicly protesting against IS policies.[183] Some even undermined IS' governance from within: for example, some teachers secretly continued teaching the pre-IS curriculum in schools.[184] But IS' grip on the territory it controlled was so intense and the punishments metered out for small objections were so extreme that women, and men, largely could not resist en masse without risking their lives. Within the group and to the civilian population, IS' gender regime appeared – and functionally was – absolute.

This means that why, where, and how women were participated in – or were excluded from – IS' proto-state structure tells us much about IS governance. It appears that there were no substantive opportunities for women to be part of new program development or to push leadership to change course on gender-related issues. But IS recruited women specifically as expansionists in roles central to their governance projects: implementing their agenda necessitated women's participation in governance structures because IS' strict gender segregation composed a core ideological tenet. And while some women were successfully recruited into these positions for lack of better options, others enthusiastically sought out these roles. As leaders and public-facing figures, women in the *hisba*, in education, the women's housing system, and in propaganda messaging provided civilian services, enforced IS rules, and modeled IS' internal gender politics to the public. They therefore constituted an essential part of IS' engagement with and oversight of populations under their control and in the outside world.

Fretilin

While IS envisioned a complete reimagining and restructuring of the state, society, and the family, Fretilin's revolutionary and governance goals were more modest, though still transformational. The organization's central aim was, according to a 1974 statement, to unite "all the nationalist and anti-colonialist forces in a common cause – authentic liberation of the people of East Timor from the colonial yolk."[185] At the core of this project, Fretilin pursued a new social order united against oppression and centered on spreading East Timorese nationalism and democracy.[186] Importantly, Fretilin viewed the social, sexual, political, and economic exploitation of women as emblematic of the colonial system it sought to throw off. As Loney notes, "The nationalist movement envisaged a conception of revolutionary femininity that was distinct

---

[183] Vale, "Defying Rules: Defying Gender?"   [184] Ibid.
[185] Quoted in Hannah Loney, *In Women's Words: Violence and Everyday Life during the Indonesian Occupation of East Timor, 1975–1999*, Asian & Asian American Studies (Sussex Academic Press, 2018): 40.
[186] Stewart, *Governing for Revolution*.

from the domestic, maternal vision of womanhood articulated within traditional and colonial social structures."[187] Fretilin recruited women into governance roles, and, while often constrained by gendered divisions of labor, women adopted program expansion as a manifestation of these revolutionary politics. Moreover, women, especially those working through Freitlin's women's wing, developed new governance projects that centered women's economic and political emancipation within the movement. Fretilin also engaged in multi-layered governance through their administrative relationships with civilians living in areas under their control.

Background

Fretilin's origins as an armed group date to Indonesia's annexation and invasion of East Timor (now Timor Leste) in 1975. At the time, East Timor, then a Portuguese colony, was undergoing a slow decolonization process during which national political parties formed and expanded. These included, among others, the Timorese Democratic Union (UDT), "a conservative party that supported continued ties with Portugal;" and Fretilin, an independence party with leftist leanings.[188] The UDT and Fretilin formed a political coalition until 1975, when Indonesia, anxious about an independent East Timor and desiring control of the entire island and its oil deposits, supported the UDT in staging a coup to overthrow the country's Portuguese governor.[189] When Portugal subsequently refused to resume planned decolonization efforts or intervene in the UDT's coup, Fretilin declared East Timor's independence. Shortly after, Indonesia invaded.

While Fretilin continued its political work rallying international partners to an independent East Timor's cause, military forces mobilized through the group's armed wing, Falintil, and launched a liberation war against Indonesian occupiers. The invasion forced thousands of civilians, Fretilin supporters, and Falintil fighters to flee into the mountains where they established *bases de apoio,* support bases where Fretilin maintained territorial control. Here, Fretilin established extensive political, administrative, and governance structures.[190] But by 1979, the Indonesian military offensive had overwhelmed the group; Fretilin went on the run, lost control of territory it had gained, but persisted as part of the broader resistance movement until the Timorese independence process began in 1999.[191]

---

[187] Loney, *In Women's Words*, 42.   [188] Stewart, *Governing for Revolution*, 169.   [189] Ibid.
[190] CAVR, *Chega! Final Report of the Commission for Reception, Truth and Reconciliation in East Timor (CAVR)* (2005), www.etan.org/news/2006/cavr.htm.
[191] Ibid.

Gendered Governance

When Fretilin declared East Timor's independence it produced a constitution for the free state. This constitution guaranteed equal rights for women and men and mandated that every citizen had both the duty and the right to fight for the country to defend its sovereignty.[192] Fretilin recruited women widely as part of its agenda for a protracted people's war: women were part of Fretilin's first Central Committee, though in very low numbers (sources suggest between one and three women participated), and a reportedly small number of women fought with Falintil on the frontlines.[193] The organization further established a large and active women's wing, the Popular Organization of Timorese Women (OPMT) which played a central role in noncombatant logistical, clandestine, diplomatic, and governance work.[194]

The OPMT's origins signal a revolutionary purpose, one that demonstrates the centrality of Fretilin's gender beliefs to its broader ideological objectives and recruitment strategies. In September 1975, Rosa "Muki" Bonaparte Soares, the OPMT's founding secretary, published a statement on the organization's behalf detailing the OPMT's purpose and place within the broader movement:

> The principal objective of women participating in the revolution is not, strictly speaking, the emancipation of women as women, but the triumph of the revolution, and consequently, the liberation of women as a social being who is the target of a double exploitation: that under the traditional conceptions and that under the colonialist conceptions.[195]

Shedding colonial manacles, the OPMT made clear, required new gender relations and embracing a 'revolutionary femininity.' And within Fretilin territory, the organization set about educating and politicizing women and socializing civilians into this rearticulated gender order. Within Fretilin's governing structure women were reportedly "encouraged to participate in political and economic decision-making," though the group's leadership encouraged them to join the OPMT instead of other bodies.[196] One key manifestation of Fretilin's ideology was therefore how women participated in the group's governance projects.

---

[192] Ibid.

[193] Irena Cristalis, Catherine Scott, and Ximena Andrade, *Independent Women: The Story of Women's Activism in East Timor* (CIIR, 2005); Nina Hall and Jacqui True, "Gender Mainstreaming in a Post-Conflict State: Toward Democratic Peace in Timor Leste?" in *Gender and Global Politics in the Asia-Pacific* (Palgrave McMillan, 2009): 159–74.

[194] Christine Mason, "Women, Violence and Nonviolent Resistance in East Timor," *Journal of Peace Research* 42, no. 6 (2005): 737–49.

[195] Rosa "Muki" Bonaparte, "Women in East Timor: Statement by Popular Organisation of Timorese Women," September 18, 1975, *Direct Action*, March 4, 1976, 7, as quoted in Loney, *In Women's Words*, 40.

[196] Stewart, *Governing for Revolution*, 181; Sara Niner, "Bisoi – A Veteran of Timor-Leste's Independence Movement," in *Women in Southeast Asian Nationalist Movements*, ed. Susan Blackburn and Helen Ting (NUS Press, 2013): 226–49.

Initially, following Indonesia's invasion, small groups of civilians including women operated in concert with local Fretilin leaders to provide for each other and rebel fighters, for example by growing and distributing food. But by 1976 Fretilin began establishing formal organizational structures in what became the *bases de apoio;* here, military commanders deferred to civilian political administrators.[197] Fretilin established a broad administration that ranged from the sub-village level up to group-level structures. Administratively Fretilin territory was divided into sectors, and within each sector political commissars oversaw administrative units such as education, housing, healthcare, and political propaganda.[198] The group operated agricultural cooperatives and instituted related economic changes, opened schools and medical centers, and held elections.[199] The political commissars worked closely with the OPMT in these areas, as women composed a significant proportion of administrative leadership and the OPMT was responsible for many programs.[200] As such, it is an exemplar of women's wings as central sites of rebel governance and of the work that civilians do to govern their communities alongside and in tandem with armed groups.

Women joined Fretilin and the OPMT in part because they viewed their participation as critical to the success of the organization's gender emancipatory agenda. The OPMT's mandate was, according to its leadership, a "people's organisation which creates opportunities for women to participate in the revolution."[201] Still, like other ideological tenets, rebellions' gendered beliefs are not impervious to shifting war conditions. In this case, Fretilin's transformative plans for gender order in and outside of the organization fell secondary to immediate war needs, particularly those concerning civilians living in its territory. As Indonesia's bombardment increased, the humanitarian crisis expanded, and more men went to fight on the front-lines, women of the OPMT took on more "traditional," service provision roles like caring for war orphans and teaching, feeding, and providing healthcare for the civilian population. Loney writes,

> This discrepancy between FRETILIN's vision for gender equality and what occurred in practice can be explained, in part, by the increasingly difficult conditions of conflict and the extremely brief period available to enact such changes. In the *zonas libertadas* [areas under FRETILIN control], the roles and responsibilities of East Timorese women were generally concerned with the practical needs of the mountain-based societies, which became increasingly structured around surviving the wartime conditions and evading attack.[202]

---

[197] CAVR, "Chega!"   [198] Ibid.   [199] Stewart, *Governing for Revolution.*
[200] CAVR, "Chega!"
[201] Hall and True, "Gender Mainstreaming in a Post-Conflict State," 162.
[202] Loney, *In Women's Words,* 51.

But importantly, within Fretilin and the OPMT, women's participation in these types of civilian-care projects were not viewed as incompatible with their broader and revolutionary gendered agenda. Instead, women imbued their service provision work with Fretilin's conception of womanhood and created new shared meanings of governance that underpinned the organization's extensive bureaucratic and administrative apparatus. Through the OPMT's work in the *bases de apoio,* women "put the values of women's emancipation into practice in the service of the people in the struggle for liberation."[203] They stressed that OPMT "members were critical to the ideological work of the struggle" and that "the objective of the participation by women in the revolution is therefore not just for the emancipation of women but the victory of revolution."[204] This work, too, became part of Fretilin's gendered model: da Silva notes that Fretilin and the OPMT, specifically, continued to "implement its revolutionary social policy" during this period.[205]

Fretilin encouraged women to work in healthcare, agricultural and goods production and distribution, and education and the group established nurseries to look after children so that more women could participate in these ways.[206] The OPMT assumed primary responsibility for education along with food provisioning and administering part of Fretilin's health system. Fretilin's Ministry of Education and Culture built education centers in areas under Fretilin control and educated OPMT women taught classes. This education system persisted under immense stress – classes reportedly only lasted around three weeks each because Indonesian bombardments forced civilians and Fretilin members to constantly flee.[207]

The group further established and organized childcare centers for war orphans, providing nutrition and teaching children.[208] Women in the OPMT were also the central organizers of and teachers within Fretilin's literacy program. Targeting both adults and children, the program taught reading, writing, and political education and, da Silva argues, "influenced the transformation of the Fretilin party into a mass popular movement [… that] laid down the foundation for the next twenty four years' resistance against the Indonesian occupation."[209] Women literacy educators outnumbered men at many points.[210]

---

[203] Maria Domingas Alves, Laura Abrantes, and Filomena Reis, *Hakerek Ho Ran (Written with Blood)* (2003), Secretaria da Promoção da Igualdade, Gabinete do Primeiro-Ministro, Díli cited in Loney, *In Women's Words*, 49.

[204] Antero Benedito da Silva, "FRETILIN Popular Education 1973–1978 and Its Relevance to Timor-Leste Today" (PhD Thesis, Tese (Doutorado em Filosofia)-University of New England, 2011), 163.

[205] Ibid., 164.   [206] CAVR, "Chega!"

[207] da Silva, "FRETILIN Popular Education 1973–1978 and Its Relevance to Timor-Leste Today."

[208] Ibid.; CAVR, "Chega!"

[209] da Silva, "FRETILIN Popular Education 1973–1978 and Its Relevance to Timor-Leste Today," 145.

[210] Loney, *In Women's Words*.

OPMT women did not only administer Fretilin's basic educational curriculum, they also developed programs focused specifically on women. This included literacy and public speaking training but also courses on women's emancipation that was intended in part, to prepare them for marriage.[211] These classes taught women, as "future brides," to challenge colonial gender attitudes and to therefore create future nationalist families with respect for women's and men's rights.[212]

Beyond its educational programming, women of the OPMT and broader Fretilin movement contributed centrally to its health campaigns. Fretilin commenced civilian health services within three months of the Indonesian invasion, combining traditional doctors and nurses with local expertise on medicinal plants and herbs.[213] The organization worked to train more health workers, many of whom were women who went on to train other women in the villages in medical expertise.[214] Women with medical backgrounds also headed Fretilin health schools. Additionally, the organization established public health campaigns educating civilians about diseases and infections.

Indonesia's annihilation campaign – which included burning down villages, airstrikes, and ground invasions – effectively ended Fretilin control of territory and governance of civilians within four years after it began. Fretilin leadership authorized civilian surrenders but asked people to remain supportive of the movement.[215] The revolutionary struggle reconstituted itself in various, less bureaucratic ways over the next few decades, and some women returned to the mountains in the 1980s to support or fight for Falintil. By 1998, a new women's wing, the Organization of Timorese Women (OMT) was founded with support from women of the OPMT.[216]

In sum, it is not possible to understand Fretilin's expansive governance campaigns and their consequences without recognizing their gendered dynamics. Women's participation in the organization, and in the OPMT, specifically, enabled the growth of service provision projects and led to the development of programs aimed specifically at civilian women. Fretilin leadership recruited women directly into these roles. But women joined the group not only because of their desire to fight Indonesia's invasion but also because of Fretilin's gendered agenda. They imbued governance work, including 'traditional' domestic work like education and healthcare provision, with Fretilin's revolutionary, gendered tenets. These attitudes and programs set the stage for Fretilin's work as a political organization in the decades to come

[211] CAVR, "Chega!"   [212] Ibid., 11.   [213] Stewart, *Governing for Revolution*.
[214] da Silva, *FRETILIN Popular Education 1973–1978 and Its Relevance to Timor-Leste Today*.
[215] CAVR, "Chega!"
[216] Niner, "Bisoi – A Veteran of Timor-Leste's Independence Movement."

and also established an organized, East Timorese women's movement that persisted through the OPMT and, later, the OMT.

Provisional IRA

The analyses presented in this section offer a fairly straightforward view of gendered rebel governance. Islamic State and FRETILIN controlled domestic territory and therefore retained responsibility for administration of civilians in these areas. But other rebel organizations effectively govern civilians without meaningful territorial control. The Provisional IRA is an example. A comparatively small, long-running rebellion that withstood the British government's attempts at decisive military victory, the Provisional IRA incompletely controlled contested territory and did so only, weakly, at the neighborhood level. Instead, this case evidences the complicated, gendered, multi-layered governance systems that often emerge when civil wars interrupt state institutional monopolies. Here, I explore these dynamics by discussing women's expansion and development of rebel governance programs from within the Provisional IRA and its affiliated groups and also the civilian women-centered governance networks in Catholic, nationalist, republican (CNR) neighborhoods[217] in Northern Ireland during the 1969–1998 conflict between IRA organizations, the British government, and pro-British paramilitaries.

Background

The conflict in Northern Ireland was born from the centuries-old struggle to free Ireland from British rule. British governance in Ireland dates back to English rule in the twelfth century, followed by the 1541 creation of the Kingdom of Ireland and the 1800 Act of Union establishing the United Kingdom of Great Britain and Ireland. The country experienced unsuccessful Irish rebellions until 1916, when the Irish Volunteers launched their insurrection – Easter Rising – intended to establish a full-island, self-governing Irish republic. Easter Rising invigorated Irish republicans – nationalists seeking to unite all of Ireland into an independent republic through military force – and prompted the IRA's (descended from the Irish Volunteers) war for Irish independence.

---

[217] CNR is a term used in Northern Ireland to encapsulate those generally opposed to British control in the country. Catholics are predominately Irish in heritage, and largely consider themselves Irish today, and they were the initiators of the 1960s civil rights movement following decades of oppression by the British government. Nationalists are those who desire a united Ireland under only Irish rule, many of whom are Catholics. Republicans are nationalists who adopt or support military force as the method for achieving a united Ireland. Cities in Northern Ireland were and remain very segregated at the neighborhood level, with CNR neighborhoods largely separate from pro-British (Protestant, unionist, loyalist) neighborhoods.

The 1921 Anglo-Irish Agreement ended the independence war by partitioning the twenty-six southern counties into the Irish Free State and leaving the most northern counties, which were those most populated by Protestant immigrants from Britain, in British hands. Many republicans saw the treaty as capitulation that betrayed the goal of a united Ireland. Their resistance triggered the 1922–1923 Irish Civil War, but they were defeated handily by the Britain-backed Free State government. In 1937, the Free State generated a new constitution and became the Republic of Ireland. The IRA continued to wage low-intensity, sporadic attacks for a united Ireland over the next four decades, though its military strength never rebounded.

The 1950s and 1960s marked periods of renewed struggle within CNR neighborhoods in Northern Ireland. Politically, economically, and socially oppressed by the British government and police, these communities launched a civil rights movement demanding an end to inequality and discrimination. These marches, protests, and strikes were met with violence from the Royal Ulster Constabulary (RUC) – the overwhelmingly Protestant police force in Northern Ireland – and armed, pro-British paramilitaries known as loyalists.[218] This violence peaked in the late 1960s, when violent confrontations led to civilian defense forces assembling in these communities as the RUC and British troops blanketed neighborhoods with military force, arrested and interned people en masse, and ignored (or colluded with) loyalist attacks on Catholics.[219] In this environment, the IRA constructed among long-time members and new recruits a reconstituted force. One former Provisional IRA member, who was later incarcerated, recalls, "It was only then, it was the people who called for the IRA" to protect them.[220] Veterans of previous iterations of the IRA, along with younger recruits, split the original group into two factions in 1969. Originally operating in defense of CNR communities, both groups began offensive campaigns in 1970. Ultimately, the Provisional IRA prevailed as the stronger, better resourced, more active, and better known organization.

Gendered governance

The Provisional IRA never meaningfully gained territory but the group exerted 'social control'[221] over many CNR communities in a variety of ways. This

---

[218] Azrini Wahidin, *Ex-Combatants, Gender and Peace in Northern Ireland* (Palgrave Macmillan, 2016).
[219] Interview with John, summer 2022; interview with Aileen, summer 2022; interview with Róisín, summer 2022. As John recalls of Derry at this time, "the city was on fucking fire." For participant confidentiality, interviews are cited using pseudonyms.
[220] Interview with Róisín, summer 2022.
[221] Jentzsch and Steele, "Social Control in Civil Wars."

included effectively preventing police and military forces from entering specific neighborhoods, making and enforcing a justice system prohibiting informing, fraternizing with British agents, drug selling, joyriding, and vandalism, and setting up courts to adjudicate violations.[222] The Provisional IRA's political wing, Sinn Féin, also provided local services to CNR civilians.[223] During the 1975 ceasefire, Sinn Féin began establishing incident and advice centers where people living in these neighborhoods could report security force harassment and violence and seek help for issues like tenet complaints and healthcare needs. Sinn Féin reportedly set up these centers to rival the government's incident centers established that same year through the Department of Health and Social Services.[224]

The Provisional IRA's belief system was relatively simple: the organization led a "people's war," one that was morally justified by British colonial violence, one that required commitment from the CNR constituency, and one in which everyone had a role.[225] The Provisional IRA sought to shift the war for a united Ireland away from one carried out by the army and into one carried out collectively by the people. The group's narratives around women's roles and opportunities were central to this ideological campaign, and women composed an important segment of the Provisional IRA's membership on and off the frontlines. The army began accepting women in 1968 and the Provisional IRA reportedly reaffirmed this decision in 1970.[226] Women likely composed around 6 percent of the organization's fighting force, but they participated much more extensively in noncombatant roles.[227]

The Provisional IRA was supported by the original IRA's women's auxiliary unit, Cumann na mBan, which took on myriad tasks including weapons and message transport, intelligence gathering, and neighborhood patrolling.[228] Women were also very involved in Sinn Féin, which first formed a Women's Coordinating Committee in 1979 and then the Sinn Féin's Women's Department

---

[222] Cyanne E. Loyle, "Rebel Courts and Rebel Legitimacy," *International Politics* (2023); Theresa O'Keefe, *Feminist Identity Development and Activism in Revolutionary Movements* (Palgrave Macmillan, 2013).

[223] Mantanock and Staniland conclude of the Provisional IRA and Sinn Féin, "There is no doubt that the two were in reality formally fused, with key Sinn Fein leaders sitting on the PIRA's Army Council, but the two publicly denied this linkage." Aila M. Matanock and Paul Staniland, "How and Why Armed Groups Participate in Elections," *Perspectives on Politics* 16, no. 3 (2018): 716.

[224] Tony Craig, "Monitoring the Peace?: Northern Ireland's 1975 Ceasefire Incident Centres and the Politicisation of Sinn Féin," *Terrorism and Political Violence* 26, no. 2 (2014): 307–19.

[225] Interview with Paul summer 2022.

[226] Dieter Reinisch, "'Cumann Na MBan' and Women in Irish Republican Paramilitary Organisations, 1969–1986," *Estudios Irlandeses* 11, (2016): 149–62.

[227] Mia Bloom, Paul Gill, and John Horgan, "Tiocfaidh Ar Mna: Women in the Provisional Irish Republican Army," *Behavioral Sciences of Terrorism and Political Aggression* 4, no. 1 (2012): 60–76.

[228] Loken, "Noncombat Participation in Rebellion."

in 1980. Gilmartin concludes that "republican women began organising within the Provisional republican movement in order to assert their own political agenda and interests in tandem with movement's overall objectives."[229] For the Provisional IRA, women's involvement – armed and otherwise – was essential evidence of their "people's war agenda." For example, a 1990s 'IRA statement' poster announces, "A woman's place is in the struggle / This is not a man's war, but a people's war and very, very much suffering has become borne by the women, be they mothers, wives, and political activists or Volunteers and the men ought to remember that without the sacrifice of women there would be no struggle at all."[230]

Women were therefore essential participants in republican organizations' formal governance structures. Women staffed many of the Sinn Féin advice centers, particularly during periods of internment when the state incarcerated without trial large numbers of men from these communities.[231] In these roles, women also developed new programs that likely would have failed to exist in their absence. For example, members of the Sinn Féin Women's Department established help centers for those who were experiencing domestic or state-perpetrated violence.[232] The Women's Department further helped establish community organizations, and in the 1980s, they convinced Sinn Féin to provide childcare or childcare funds for members so that they could participate in organizational events.[233] The organization highlighted that women bore the brunt of British violence in Northern Ireland and that, as such, their participation in resistance and rebellion evidenced the total nature of the republican campaign.[234]

Women also took part in the Provisional IRA's policing initiatives. O'Keefe notes, "In the absence of a trusted police force, the IRA fashioned itself into the local policing body in republican areas," engaging in both political and civil policing.[235] She further concludes that the Provisional IRA police were "used as

[229] Niall Gilmartin, "Feminism, Nationalism and the Re-ordering of Post-War Political Strategies: The Case of the Sinn Féin Women's Department," *Irish Political Studies* 32, no. 2 (2017): 269.
[230] "A Woman's Place is in the Struggle … " Irish Republican Army, est. 1990s. Linen Hall Library, Northern Ireland Political Collection, Troubled Images.
[231] Interview with Mary, summer 2022.
[232] Gilmartin, "Feminism, Nationalism and the Re-ordering of Post-War Political Strategies."
[233] Ibid.
[234] See, for example, Sinn Féin Women's Department, *Women in Struggle* (1994). Linen Hall Library, Northern Ireland Political Collection, Box: "Women." Gilmartin contends that "the roots of the Women's Department resided solely with the agency of republican women themselves with little input from the male-led leadership" (Gilmartin, "Feminism, Nationalism and the Re-ordering of Post-War Political Strategies," 275). At the same time, one former Provisional IRA member suggested that Gerry Adams, originally an IRA leader who became the head of Sinn Féin, was partially responsible for the department's establishment through his advocacy of the organization (field notes, summer 2022).
[235] O'Keefe, *Feminist Identity Development and Activism in Revolutionary Movements*, 71.

a tool to enhance the image of the IRA in republican areas and to maintain a strong level of support within the community for all of its operations."[236] This including punishment beatings, knee-capping, and executions for disloyal members and civilian informers, but also local law enforcement against offenses like drug trafficking, sexual abuse, and drunk driving. Women participated in some of these policing and punishment activities.[237] For example, the high-profile abduction and disappearance of civilian Jean McConville in 1972 was reportedly carried out by a group of women and men.[238] Some women also transported marked men and women to their deaths and were present at, and may have participated in, punishment murders.[239] Women civilians were reportedly among the most supportive of the Provisional IRA's "law and order" governance style: in 1991 when the group decided to stop policing in West Belfast, over 200 women successfully organized a protest demanding that they return.[240]

Women, both members of IRA groups and civilians, also formed what they called "hen patrols," a form of all-women policing and territorial governance. British Army soldiers blanketed CNR neighborhoods, raiding and trashing homes, brutalizing inhabitants, and arresting men and women without charges, often during the night.[241] When British Army soldiers would patrol, groups of woman who rotated by shift would follow them and alert civilians and IRA members to their presence by banging bid lids and blowing whistles.[242] Some of these women were shot and killed by British forces.[243]

At the same time, Provisional IRA and Sinn Féin governance was not extensive and civilians in CNR areas were largely "abandoned" by the state: they were actively dissuaded from turning to the government for resources by high levels of state violence through wanton arrests, raids, assaults, denial of services, and collusion with loyalist paramilitary groups.[244] The government never fully stepped in to support civilians who were losing their homes, safety, and family members to bombs, arrests, and street violence.[245] In this context, what arose in many CNR areas was not always or only rebel governance, but civilian service provision networks that reflect the complexity of governing

---

[236] Ibid., 72.   [237] Ibid.   [238] Ibid.
[239] Patrick Radden Keefe, *Say Nothing: A True Story of Murder and Memory in Northern Ireland* (William Collins, 2018).
[240] O'Keefe, *Feminist Identity Development and Activism in Revolutionary Movements.*
[241] Cyanne E. Loyle, Christopher Sullivan, and Christian Davenport, "The Northern Ireland Research Initiative: Data on the Troubles from 1968 to 1998," *Conflict Management and Peace Science* 31, no. 1 (2014): 94–106.
[242] O'Keefe, *Feminist Identity Development and Activism in Revolutionary Movements.*
[243] Monica McWilliams, "Struggling for Peace and Justice: Reflections on Women's Activism in Northern Ireland," *Journal of Women's History* 7, no. 1 (1995): 13–39.
[244] Interview with Conor, winter 2022.   [245] Ibid.

during war. Provisional IRA and Sinn Féin members, clandestine auxiliary participants, and civilians in CNR communities worked in overlapping systems in this respect. One republican activist recalls, "it was self-help, you had to do it, and they organized themselves."[246] This network functioned, principally, around women.

Women were "key players" in these CNR communities' "self-reliant" governance systems, in part because civilians and republican activists "were treated with contempt" by and harbored "profound distrust of" the state.[247] In Belfast, women organized housing for families burned out of their homes by loyalist paramilitaries, fed those struggling to meet basic needs, organized support networks for republican prisoners' families, and ran Irish language and educational programs.[248] In the early 1970s, sectarian violence forced nearly 30,000 from their homes at gunpoint, because of arson, or otherwise coercively, creating the then-largest refugee community in Western Europe since the end of World War II.[249] Women organized housing and care for thousands in the face of such deprivation. As one woman, a dedicated (civilian) republican, summarized, "I've always tried to analyze what we are. We are a community, but we were more than that. We were the welfare, we were the health board, we were the transport, we were the babysitting service." She continued,

> Swear to God, the Brits would never have broken our network … they just would never beat us. They'd never. How could you beat a network of women? … There ain't nothing that they could throw at us that we couldn't cope with. The support mechanism that this road [Falls Road] and other areas sat on, second to none.[250]

In 1970, the British army declared a "curfew" in the neighborhoods along the Falls Road in CNR West Belfast. The military sealed the perimeter in order to conduct home raids. They prevented food deliveries from entering this zone, which constituted about 3,000 homes, for nearly three days. Women brought milk, bread, and other rations on foot to those living inside the area, breaking the through military blockade and effectively ending the curfew.[251]

Another illustrative example is the Relatives Action Committees (RACs), first established in 1976 by Catholic civilian women primarily from West Belfast to support families of those interned and otherwise incarcerated.

---

[246] Ibid.   [247] Interview with Conor, winter 2022.
[248] Interview with Aileen, summer 2022; interview with Róisín, summer 2022; author field notes, summer 2017 and 2022.
[249] McWilliams, "Struggling for Peace and Justice," 25.
[250] Interview with Aileen, summer 2022.
[251] McWilliams, "Struggling for Peace and Justice."

Several such local committees proliferated across the country as incarceration increased. And while the RACs organized mass demonstrations and political actions, they also stepped in to care for the material and emotional needs of republican prisoners' families.[252] They, along with Sinn Féin representatives, began international diplomatic campaigns, traveling to the United States, Canada, and Britain, meeting with legislators and advocating for republican prisoners and their families.[253] As the state stepped back or actively conspired against them, women stepped in to govern and to mark a place for themselves in the "people's war" against British violence. As in the other two cases discussed here, women's governance contributions to the Provisional IRA, formally and informally, appear hugely consequential. Moreover, civilian women's governance work supporting community members and their other activism against British abuses helped maintain the movement. As O'Keefe concludes, "Without women's work, communities would have disintegrated entirely, as would the republican campaign."[254]

Dynamics of Gendered Governance across Cases

In this Element, I argue that rebel governance is gendered in ways that affect these institutions' development, content, and implementation and the relationships between armed groups and civilian populations. Each case examined here – IS, Fretilin, and the Provisional IRA – illustrates different components of this framework. But all three offer context and support for this argument by illustrating how women's recruitment and participation in governance formally and informally, helps explain the materiality and scope of these projects. Moreover, these descriptive analyses demonstrate that it is not only the presence of women working in noncombatant roles but the internal and external gender dynamics of armed groups that shape governance institutions. Across cases, governance projects also appear to grow in scale and ambition as more women become participants in rebels' activities, and women's wings are influential players in this administrative landscape. Finally, these examples make clear that it is not only 'rebel women' but also activists and civilian women whose contributions help extend and develop nonstate governance of their communities during civil wars.

These brief investigations do not encompass every aspect of women's contributions to rebel governance. Given known patterns of erasure of women's noncombatant work within rebel groups and in conflict-affected areas, it is likely that women originate, change, and influence governance projects in ways we simply cannot yet see. Still, evidence from these three cases

---

[252] Ibid.; O'Keefe, *Feminist Identity Development and Activism in Revolutionary Movements.*
[253] McWilliams, "Struggling for Peace and Justice."
[254] O'Keefe, *Feminist Identity Development and Activism in Revolutionary Movements*, 24.

demonstrates the utility of the framework that I introduce in Section 3. These analyses illustrate that attention to the gender dynamics of recruitment into and organization of governance roles, expansion and development of governance institutions, and the realities of multi-layered governance provides evidence of and mechanisms for consequential relationships between rebel institutions, women's involvement in rebellion, and women's experiences of conflict more broadly. Moreover, this approach helps explain cross-conflict patterns in the gendered, global governance landscape.

5 Implications and Legacies of Gendered Governance

In 2019, IS' governance programs collapsed with the group's final territorial defeat in Baghuz al-Fawqani, Syria. Over the previous year, remaining members of the organization had fled from city to city as the Syrian Defence Forces (SDF) – a primarily Kurdish group backed by the multinational anti-IS military coalition – expelled them from their once-held territories. Islamic State fighters took their families and other civilians with them as they attempted to out-run the counter-insurgents, culminating in the last stand in Baghuz al-Fawqani wherein thousands of civilians and fighters were forced out under protracted siege. The SDF then detained suspected IS fighters and some family members while transferring thousands of civilians to internally-displaced persons (IDP) camps in the northern part of the country. This included al-Hol, which ballooned in size to hold over 70,000 individuals.[255] al-Hol is administered, in name, by the SDF, but, in reality, it was and remains at least partially governed by IS members and supporters.

al-Hol is mostly populated by women and children. And while the camp is ostensibly intended to house civilians displaced by IS, much of its population remains committed to IS' ideology and many individuals are women who previously joined the organization. In al-Hol and other camps, women continue to govern other women according to IS' rules through what Vale calls a "continuation in ideals and function of al-Khansā [sic]" and other *hisba* brigades.[256] Improperly pious dress or behavior, including renouncing support for IS or meeting with aid workers, is punished, often physically. Some who refuse to attend Qur'anic courses are violently lashed. Women who once followed IS to Baghuz al-Fawqani have now "erected their own *shari'a* 'court' modelled on IS' judicial system" within the camps.[257] Stripped of territorial control and devolved from a cohesive rebellion to a loose network of allegiants, IS continues to govern what the Syrian Observatory for Human

---

[255] UNICEF, *Unwanted, Exploited and Abused: Tens of Thousands of Children in Al-Hol Camp and Several Parts of Syria in Limbo amid Dire Humanitarian Needs* (2019).
[256] Vale, *Women in Islamic State*, 6.   [257] Ibid., 7.

Rights deems the "al-Hawl mini state [sic]."[258] What's more, it is women's active participation that makes this continued governance possible.

In this Element, I have argued that rebel governance is gendered and that these gendered dynamics affect the content and execution of governance institutions. These arguments are supported by descriptive cross-conflict data on governance programs and women's participation in armed groups and by evidence from three diverse organizations – IS, Fretilin, and the Provisional IRA. But research on the gender dynamics of rebel governance is still emergent. And as the IS case discussed above suggests, there is much still to know about the causes, practices, and consequences of rebels' gendered governance during and after war. In this section, I consider what we still do not know about women, gender and rebel governance; what my research has to say about the consequences of gendered governance for rebel groups, political institutions, and societies; and what gendered governance might mean for reintegration and transition for rebels in the "post-fighting" period. I also reflect throughout on how this project may ground future paths of research in these areas.

What Can We Know about Gendered Governance?

First, this Element provides a framework for interrogating rebellions' internal gender dynamics that may usefully bolster future projects. For example, this work offers theoretical reasons to expect that there might be patterns across groups wherein certain tenets of rebels' ideologies are most likely to result in specific forms of women's participation, including specific types of governance. This is certainly true at the most aggregate levels – left-leaning groups with relatively gender-liberatory regimes appear most likely to recruit women into leadership roles, for instance.[259] But we may be able to see these trends at a more nuanced level, including *how* women participate in rebel governance.

Here is an example. The case study data presented in this project make clear that there is a relationship between organizations' internal gender dynamics and the kinds of governance projects women take on. Groups with more restrictive gender norms, for example, appear to offer fewer opportunities for women to engage in project development. While case study examination of individual rebellions' gendered strategies will provide the most detailed information, my research suggests the possibility of a typological set that links specific gender beliefs and recruitment strategies at the rebel leadership level (inputs) with specific types of women's governance participation (outputs) across

[258] Syrian Observatory for Human Rights, "21 murders so far in 2021 | Iraqi refugee shot dead in 'Al-Hawl mini-state'" (February 21, 2021), www.syriahr.com/en/205955/.

[259] Loken and Matfess, "Introducing the Women's Activities in Armed Rebellion (WAAR) Project, 1946–2015."

organizations. For example, preliminary analyses of the WAAR Project's qualitative data on women's wings suggests that rebel groups that mandate women's segregation from men in public spaces are most likely to include all-women's policing units. Such a typology would tell us a great deal about the relationships between rebels' gender dynamics and rebel governance.

Research in this area may also develop cross-conflict and contextual explanations for variation in gendered rebel governance across armed groups. The descriptive relationships illustrated in Section 2 suggest a remarkable association between organizations engaged in governance institutions and women's participation in noncombatant roles, but future scholarship can use the framework developed in this Element, and the typological suggestion given above, to evaluate these trends when we consider covariates as explanatory factors. In this vein, this Element provides the infrastructure for deeper interrogation of governance institutions individually and comparatively: future research may study gendered variation within and across governance project types.

Up to this point, I've conceptualized and discussed the gendered dynamics of rebel governance as related to women's participation in or contributions to armed group activities. That is the focus of this study. But another important dynamic related to women's integration within rebel groups is the role of gendered beliefs in rebels' ideological governance projects. It is not only how women gender governance that matters, but also how rebels' governance may intend to change, transform, or entrench state and social conceptions of gender order. There is tremendous opportunity for researchers to know more about *how rebels govern gender,* within their groups and within communities under their control. Burgeoning research in this field examines rebel governance of marriage,[260] and some are beginning to explore when, how, and why rebel groups challenge or entrench civilian gender norms during war.[261] I suggest that the dynamics of gendered governance explored in this Element are likely related to these governance outputs that regulate gender norms and rules.

For example, the Communist Party of the Philippines (CPP) and its military wing, the New People's Army (NPA), recruited women widely in all roles as part of its revolutionary agenda.[262] This agenda included remaking women's roles in a liberatory, anti-colonial society. The CPP instituted this vision through

---

[260] Matfess, "In Love and at War"; Jenny Hedström, "Weddings Amidst War: The Intimate and Insurgent Politics of Marriage," *Citizenship Studies* (2024): 1–15. DOI: 10.1080/13621025.2024.2321721; Keshab Giri, "Rebel Governance of Marriage and Sexuality: An Intersectional Approach," *International Studies Quarterly* 67, no. 2 (2023): 1–12.

[261] Tessa Devereaux Evans, "To Have and to Hold: The Determinants of Insurgent Gender Governance," *Paper Presented at the 2023 Meeting of Conflict Research Society,* London.

[262] Belinda A. Aquino, "Filipino Women and Political Engagement," *Review of Women's Studies* 4, no. 1 (1994): 32–53.

territorial control and a governance system that included administrative regulation of many types, including of gendered relationships. The CPP's *Notes on the Party's Rules on Courtship and Marriage* (est. late 1970s-early 1980s) specifies that the group must approve courtship and marriage for group members and that love for the revolution and its proletariat tenets must supersede all else.[263] This rule applied to members courting or marrying civilians outside the organization as well. The CPP argues that proletarian marriage is based on the love and equal rights of women and men and that the group's governance of this practice is intended as a method of guaranteeing women's equality.[264] As this case illustrates, how women participate in rebel organizations likely reflects and/or is reflected, at least in part, in how those organizations govern gender, as both constitute essential parts of rebellion's preferred gender orders. These relationships demand scholarly attention.

Consequences of Gendered Governance

Rebel governance is a discrete achievement during war, one that can cultivate important resourcing relationships and demonstrate legitimacy and authority domestically and abroad. But an enduring set of questions in the scholarship on rebellions asks how rebel governance affects other group outcomes. Given the findings articulated in this Element, how might the gendered dynamics of rebel governance inform broader rebel trajectories?

First, research on the effects of administering governance on rebel successes is limited. Stewart evaluates the expectation that rebel governance enhances military strength, an important factor in explaining rebels' outcomes. She finds that, despite the expectation that rebel governance will generate favor, legitimacy, information, resources, and recruits from civilians such that the group's military capabilities are improved, rebel organizations providing services do not appear militarily superior to their counterparts.[265] But other research identifies clear advantages for governing rebels. For example, Heger and Jung conclude that when rebels provide social services they are most likely to secure peace negotiations with the state because of a causal governance logic: governance efforts secure civilian support for the group, which deters spoilers from breaking off into their own factions, which, in turn, increases government willingness to negotiate with well-supported, stable challengers.[266]

---

[263] "Notes on the Party's Rules on Courtship and Marriage," n.d. Antoinette Raquiza Collection on the Philippine Left, 1–50, COLL00197, International Institute of Social History.

[264] Ibid.

[265] Megan A. Stewart, "Rebel Governance: Military Boon or Military Bust?" *Conflict Management and Peace Science* 37, no. 1 (2019): 16–38.

[266] Heger and Jung, "Negotiating with Rebels."

A clear finding of my analyses is that women's participation is often a central part of service provision, of generating civilian support for rebels, and of the interactions between these two projects. While extant research evaluates the beneficial effects that women frontline fighters' participation can have on group survival, securing peace negotiations, or outright victory,[267] the framework articulated in this Element offers avenues for theorizing how women's noncombatant work may influence these kinds of outcomes. Giri and Haer write about frontline fighters, for example, that women are a "crucial human resource [...] recruiting women can produce significant strategic and political utility by attracting more national and international attention, as well as by strengthening the relationship between the rebel group and the civilian population."[268] My research suggests that some of these factors may be even more pronounced for women noncombatants and that their contributions to governance institutions can be distinctively consequential for rebels' relationships with civilians and their organizational capacities.

Second, anecdotal evidence suggests that how women participate in rebel governance can go on to inform post-fighting politics. In many conflict-affected areas, rebel leaders and the broader political and civilian apparatuses push to return society to "normal," including to pre-conflict gender roles.[269] But because women's participation in rebel groups often challenges traditional notions of women's place in society, it can sometimes change attitudes about gender among women themselves, their male counterparts, and rebel leadership.[270] Rebel leaders in Uganda and Zimbabwe, for example, explained that their decisions to promote women in formal politics at the end of war was because of how women's frontline, noncombatant, and leadership contributions during conflict demonstrated women's capabilities.[271] This effect may extend to governance work, specifically.

For example, in South Sudan, many women who joined the Sudan People's Liberation Movement/Army- In Opposition (SPLM/A-IO) were involved "in organising the transport of people and supplies to and from rebel held areas, managing refugee community collective mobilisation and funding, and organising local administration and justice systems."[272] They brought these and other skills to SPLM/A-IO that they had honed during previous rebellions, including

---

[267] Brannon, Thomas, and DiBlasi, "Fighting for Peace?"; Braithwaite and Ruiz, "Female Combatants, Forced Recruitment, and Civil Conflict Outcomes."

[268] Giri and Haer, "Female Combatants and Durability of Civil War," 2.

[269] Brannon, "Celebrated and Sidelined."

[270] Ibid.; Tanya Lyons, *Guns and Guerilla Girls: Women in the Zimbabwean National Liberation Struggle* (Africa World Press, 2004).

[271] Ibid.

[272] Nicki Kindersley and Øystein H. Rolandsen, "Civil War on a Shoestring: Rebellion in South Sudan's Equatoria Region," *Civil Wars* 19, no. 3 (2017): 10.

in the rebel group-turned-government from which the IO ultimately split and later negotiated with, the Sudan People's Liberation Movement (SPLM). The SPLM/A-IO also included a noncombatant Women's League and a National Committee for Gender and Women Empowerment within their parallel government structure, and their delegation for the 2014 peace talks with the SPLM involved three women among its ten members.[273] This included Sophia Pal Gai, who, in her words, "was active in women's empowerment programs of the Southern Sudan Relief Association (SSRA) which was the relief wing [humanitarian outreach wing] of the SPLM movement" before joining SPLM/A-IO.[274] The other women in the delegation were Banguot Amumm, a frontline fighter, and Rebecca Garang, a rebel and the wife of the SPLM's deceased founder.

Pal Gai recalls that her experience administering to civilians from within the SPLM, and later the SPLM/A-IO, shaped her and her comrades' views of women's participation in rebellion and the post-conflict period and of their contributions to the peace negotiation process:

> Together with other women we presented a position paper and aired out our political views at the negotiation table covering issues that are critical to women such as women's right to life, peace and security, health services, access to information, and humanitarian assistance. The issues we aired and others were included in the peace agreement. A big win for women also included securing the 25% affirmative action quota in the peace agreement for women's inclusion in all government spheres.[275]

The agreements also enshrined "equitable representation" of the SPLM Women's League and other wings within the government's Political Bureau.[276] This is, of course, only one case and it is possible that such a relationship between governance activities, political representation, and peace negotiation do not translate more broadly. Few negotiation processes include women in rebel delegations: between 1990 and 2014, women were signatories to only 10 percent of peace agreements (including from rebel and state delegations).[277] But the SPLM/A-IO

---

[273] Sudan Tribune, "SPLM-IO Women League Elects Their Chairperson," (December 23, 2015), https://sudantribune.com/article55848/.

[274] Julia Akur Majot, "On the Couch: A Conversation with Hon. Sophia Pal Gai, Former Minister of Water Resources and Irrigation in South Sudan," *Andariya* (November 28, 2022), www .andariya.com/post/on-the-couch-with-hon-sophia-pal-gai-the-former-south-sudan-minister-of-water-and-gender. Pal Gai was also elected head of the SPLM/A-IO's Women's League in 2015. Her name is reported as "Pak Gai" or "Pal Gai" in separate sources; I use Pal Gai because this is how she refers to herself in this interview.

[275] Ibid., 1.

[276] Agreement on the Reunification of the SPLM (2015), 7. https://peacemaker.un.org/southsudan-arusha-agreement2015.

[277] Jana Krause, Werner Krause, and Piia Bränfors, "Women's Participation in Peace Negotiations and the Durability of Peace," *International Interactions* 44, no. 6 (2018): 985–1016.

case demonstrates how women involved in rebel governance activities can go on to advocate for female civilians and political participants when afforded the opportunities to participate in formal political processes.

Socio-political Legacies

Another under-studied question in rebel governance research concerns the long-term effects of governance projects: and what are the lasting effects of rebel governance on political institutions and societies?[278] My research underscores a related question: what are the long-term implications of rebel governance, and how are these effects shaped, or not, by the gender dynamics therein? What can rebel groups' gender dynamics and the correlations between women's participation and rebel governance institutions tell us about post-conflict orders?

This is a relatively nascent field, but research on rebel governance suggests that such efforts can profoundly reshape social and political institutions during and after war. Huang, for example, demonstrates that rebel governance is more likely in cases where rebels depend heavily on the civilian population and that this can trigger political transformation among civilians, mobilizing the population to recognize the state's shortcomings, demand changes, and ultimately even push a country toward responsive democratization in the post-war period.[279] Rebel institutions may also be "sticky," particularly when they are superior to the state's efforts, and persist even if a rebellion fails, concedes, or negotiates a peace deal. As the SPLM/A-IO example above demonstrates, many peace agreements merge rebel institutions with the government's. Some research on the legacies of rebel governance focus relatedly on judicial inheritances: Loyle, for instance, demonstrates how post-conflict rule of law can adopt components of rebel judiciaries.[280]

Other research in this area focuses on the electoral politics of formerly rebel political parties. Many rebel organizations hold elections and/or operate political wings that participate in formal politics in some capacity during conflict. These wings often provide rebel groups a foothold in "legitimate" politics through which they transition into legal political parties during and after war. Indeed, rebels who held elections or participated in the state's elections during war may become better organized political parties in post-conflict periods.[281] But even rebellions without political wings join the formal political fray. In either case,

---

[278] Cyanne E. Loyle, Kathleen Gallagher Cunningham, Reyko Huang, and Danielle F. Jung, "New Directions in Rebel Governance Research," *Perspectives on Politics* (2021): 1–13.

[279] Reyko Huang, *The Wartime Origins of Democratization: Civil War, Rebel Governance, and Political Regimes* (Cambridge University Press, 2016).

[280] Loyle, "Rebel Justice during Armed Conflict."

[281] Loyle et al., "New Directions in Rebel Governance Research," 272.

rebel governance efforts may contribute greatly to rebel-to-party transitions: "Candidates who participated in rebel governance have a record to run on, leading to governance experience and potentially higher quality candidates."[282]

Rebel governance's gendered dynamics may affect these social and political legacies. Research on the gendered aspects of war's long shadow demonstrates that women's participation in rebellion has relevant post-conflict implications. Brannon, for example, concludes that rebel parties are more likely to run women candidates than other parties in a bid to distance themselves from violence and legitimize their politics.[283] And elsewhere, she finds that, in a study of African rebel parties from 1970 to 2020, parties in which women held political leadership roles during war were more likely to elect women to office than other rebel parties.[284] As discussed in Sections 2 and 3, governance work within rebellion sometimes involves women's participation in noncombatant leadership. This is particularly true of programs organized by rebel women's wings, like the OPMT or Sinn Féin's Women's Department. These experiences may resource women leaders with skills, backgrounds, and records that are attractive to voters, helping to explain why these women perform uniquely well during elections. For example, since the peace agreement in 1998, Sinn Féin has had the highest level of women elected to Northern Ireland's legislature of any party, and they operate an informal gender quota for contested seats.[285] Developing the theoretical framework to explain these relationships more fully and assessing these dynamics empirically may be a rich avenue for future scholarship.

Women's backgrounds in governance-related leadership may be deciding factors not only in voter choices, but also in political appointments. For example, when the SPLM became South Sudan's autonomous government in 2005, Sophia Pal Gai (before she joined the SPLM/A-IO) was appointed to the commission of war disabled, widows, and orphans due to her prior work in administering humanitarian aid. She later became the SPLM's Minister of Water Resources and Irrigation.[286]

Women's participation in rebel governance may also offer promising economic and social benefits to post-conflict societies. During the Nepalese Civil War, for instance, Maoist rebels trained over one thousand health workers. Most

---

[282] Ibid.

[283] Elizabeth L. Brannon, "Women's Political Representation in African Rebel Parties," *The Journal of Politics* 85, no. 3 (2023): 812–25.

[284] Elizabeth L. Brannon, "The Election of Former Rebel Women," *Journal of Peace Research* 85, no. 3 (2023): 1–16.

[285] Neil Matthews and Sophie Whiting, "'To the Surprise of Absolutely No One': Gendered Political Leadership Change in Northern Ireland," *The British Journal of Politics and International Relations* 24, no. 2 (2022): 224–42.

[286] Majot, "On the Couch."

measurable health outcomes improved during that war, a counterintuitive finding considering the devastating infrastructural impact of armed conflict.[287] At
least one study attributes these improvements to the Maoist training and expansion of health services, suggesting that aspects of rebel governance like service
provision could carry over into the post-conflict period if these health workers
were integrated into the "legitimate" healthcare space.[288]

Moreover, in the Nepalese case, it was women health workers who expressed
the greatest interest in integrating into the mainstream health sector.[289] In their
survey of 197 health workers, Devkotaa and van Teijlingenb found that while
the vast majority of people joined the Maoist rebellion's health system because
of their political beliefs, 72 percent of women workers supported joining formal
health services.[290] This is compared to only 55 percent of male workers – the
authors conclude that women's "higher motivation could be attributed to their
perceptions of having fewer job opportunities compared to their male
counterparts."[291] This is an important finding considering the associations
identified between rebels providing healthcare and women's participation in
noncombatant positions.

How women participate in a rebellion, then, may offer new opportunities
beneficial for women outside of war. In this case, women who may likely be
otherwise excluded from the workforce received professional training that they
could, theoretically, translate into formal labor participation. Some types of
rebel governance, therefore, may provide opportunities and skill-sets for reinte-
grating individuals into civilian society, for improving civilian outcomes, and
possibly even for increasing women's access to the formal economy. This is an
area for future research – how do women's experiences and rebellion-developed
expertise translate into the non-conflict space? Are women not engaged in
frontline fighting structurally impeded from this form of integration, or might
rebel governance experience translate into social and economic changes in post-
conflict periods? What may explain variation across cases?

The question of how rebels' gender dynamics may color the long-term
legacies of rebel governance is a conceptual one, as we simply do not yet
have much data, anecdotal or otherwise, on governance efforts' long-term
implications. But because the gendered dynamics of governance are associated
with practices and content of governance institutions during conflict, it may also

---

[287] Bhimsen Devkota and Edwin R. van Teijlingen, "Understanding Effects of Armed Conflict on
Health Outcomes: The Case of Nepal," *Conflict and Health* 4 (2010): 1–8.

[288] Ibid.

[289] Bhimsen Devkota and Edwin van Teijlingen, "Demystifying the Maoist Barefoot Doctors of
Nepal," *Medicine, Conflict, and Survival* 26, no. 2 (2010): 108–23.

[290] Ibid.   [291] Ibid., 114.

inform transitions into post-war periods. Women's wings, in particular, may outlive rebellions' militant apparatuses and continue working in governing roles after fighting ends. This appears to occur in large part because of the opportunity for political mobilization that women's wings offer as well as the gendered social networks women's wings build with the civilian population and civil society during and after war.

Fretilin's revolutionary approach to gender and gendered governance, for example, shaped the broader Timorese independence movement well after the rebellion itself ended; Niner and Loney call the OPMT the "kernel of an East Timorese women's movement," as the group outlived Fretilin's army and well-established administrators and organizers continued their roles as activists and mobilizers within the broader resistance.[292] Former leaders of the OPMT became the founders of other women's associations, some of which participated in international diplomatic efforts throughout the 1980s and 1990s.[293] In other cases, women's wings that provide the loci for rebels governance programs transition into civil society organizations after war, continuing their engagement with civilian populations through service provision, political activism, and lobbying the government for policy developments.

Conclusion

This Element addresses a lacuna between robust but often isolated research fields: research addressing rebel governance and legitimation practices and scholarship focusing on women's participation in rebellion. Research on rebel governance often overlooks women's involvement. A burgeoning scholarship demonstrates the effects of women's participation on operational behaviors and rebel outcomes like conflict duration and victory but under-values or ignores how gender shapes rebels' noncombatant activities and engagement with civilians. This project develops a framework for understanding and studying gendered rebel governance and explores how women's participation is related to and informs governance institutions. I demonstrate that rebels' internal gender dynamics and women's contributions are important for understanding the development and delivery of rebel governance projects. Future research can examine these relationships more deeply and explore the boundaries of the arguments advanced here.

---

[292] Sara Louise Niner and Hannah Loney, "The Women's Movement in Timor-Leste and Potential for Social Change," *Politics & Gender* 16, no. 3 (2020): 88.
[293] Ibid.

Acknowledgments

I am very grateful to my interlocutors in Northern Ireland and to the staff and members of Tar Anall for their assistance, time, and research support. I also thank series editors Tiffany Barnes and Diana O'Brian for their support, feedback, and encouragement, as well as Elizabeth Brannon, Hilary Matfess, Laura Huber, Summer Lindsey, Lindsey Goldberg, Sumin Lee, Abbey Steele, Juan Masullo, Imke Harbers, Jessica Soedirgo, and the anonymous reviewers for their comments on drafts of and advice about this project. Penelope Bollini and Cecilia Cavero provided excellent research assistance with the cross-conflict data analysis, and I am relatedly thankful for Jenna Norosky's work on the Women's Armed Activities in Rebellion (WAAR) Project. Many thanks to Aaron Zelin and Aymenn Jawad Al-Tamimi for their work translating Islamic State (IS) documents into English, as I found these invaluable resources for this research. I am grateful for comments and suggestions from participants at the Conflict Research Society 2022 annual meeting, International Studies Association 2023 annual meeting, the University of Washington International Security Colloquium, and the Conflict Research Network at the University of Amsterdam. And I am grateful to Amy, for her love and support.

Cambridge Elements

Gender and Politics

Tiffany D. Barnes
University of Texas at Austin

Tiffany D. Barnes is Professor of Government at University of Texas at Austin. She is the author of *Women, Politics, and Power: A Global Perspective* (Rowman & Littlefield, 2007) and, award-winning, *Gendering Legislative Behavior* (Cambridge University Press, 2016). Her research has been funded by the National Science Foundation (NSF) and recognized with numerous awards. Barnes is the former president of the Midwest Women's Caucus and founder and director of the Empirical Study of Gender (EGEN) network.

Diana Z. O'Brien
Washington University in St. Louis

Diana Z. O'Brien is the Bela Kornitzer Distinguished Professor of Political Science at Washington University in St. Louis. She specializes in the causes and consequences of women's political representation. Her award-winning research has been supported by the NSF and published in leading political science journals. O'Brien has also served as a Fulbright Visiting Professor, an associate editor at *Politics & Gender*, the president of the Midwest Women's Caucus, and a founding member of the EGEN network.

About the Series

From campaigns and elections to policymaking and political conflict, gender pervades every facet of politics. Elements in Gender and Politics features carefully theorized, empirically rigorous scholarship on gender and politics. The Elements both offer new perspectives on foundational questions in the field and identify and address emerging research areas.

Cambridge Elements ≡

Gender and Politics

Elements in the Series

Printed in the United States
by Baker & Taylor Publisher Services